AF469264

ART FOR EVERYONE

CONTEMPORARY LITHOGRAPHS LTD

Ruth Artmonsky

ART FOR EVERYONE

CONTEMPORARY LITHOGRAPHS LTD

Ruth Artmonsky

First Published 2007
Artmonsky Arts
Reprinted 2010

ISBN 978-1-85149-627-3

British Library Cataloguing-in-Publication Data:
A catalogue record for this book is available from the British Library

Designed by Webb & Webb Design Limited
Set in Monotype Fournier & Monotype Ultra Bodoni

Printed in China
for the Antique Collectors' Club Ltd, Woodbridge, Suffolk

page 6 *Newhaven Harbour*, Eric Ravilious (detail)

Page 8 *Landscape of the Megaliths*, Paul Nash (detail)

Page 10 *Charade*, Barnett Freedman (detail)

ACKNOWLEDGEMENTS

To my dear daughters, Stella and Becky,
whose very existence has kept me going.

With thanks to
Ann Baer, who at 93 applied her sharp mind generously, searching back through her amazing career, to flesh out my account.

Hugh Fowler-Wright who, fighting his own battles, had the kindness to spare me time with informed and encouraging e-mails.

Owen Davies, who persevered in dealing with the massive V&A collection and machinery, to extricate the relevant images for me.

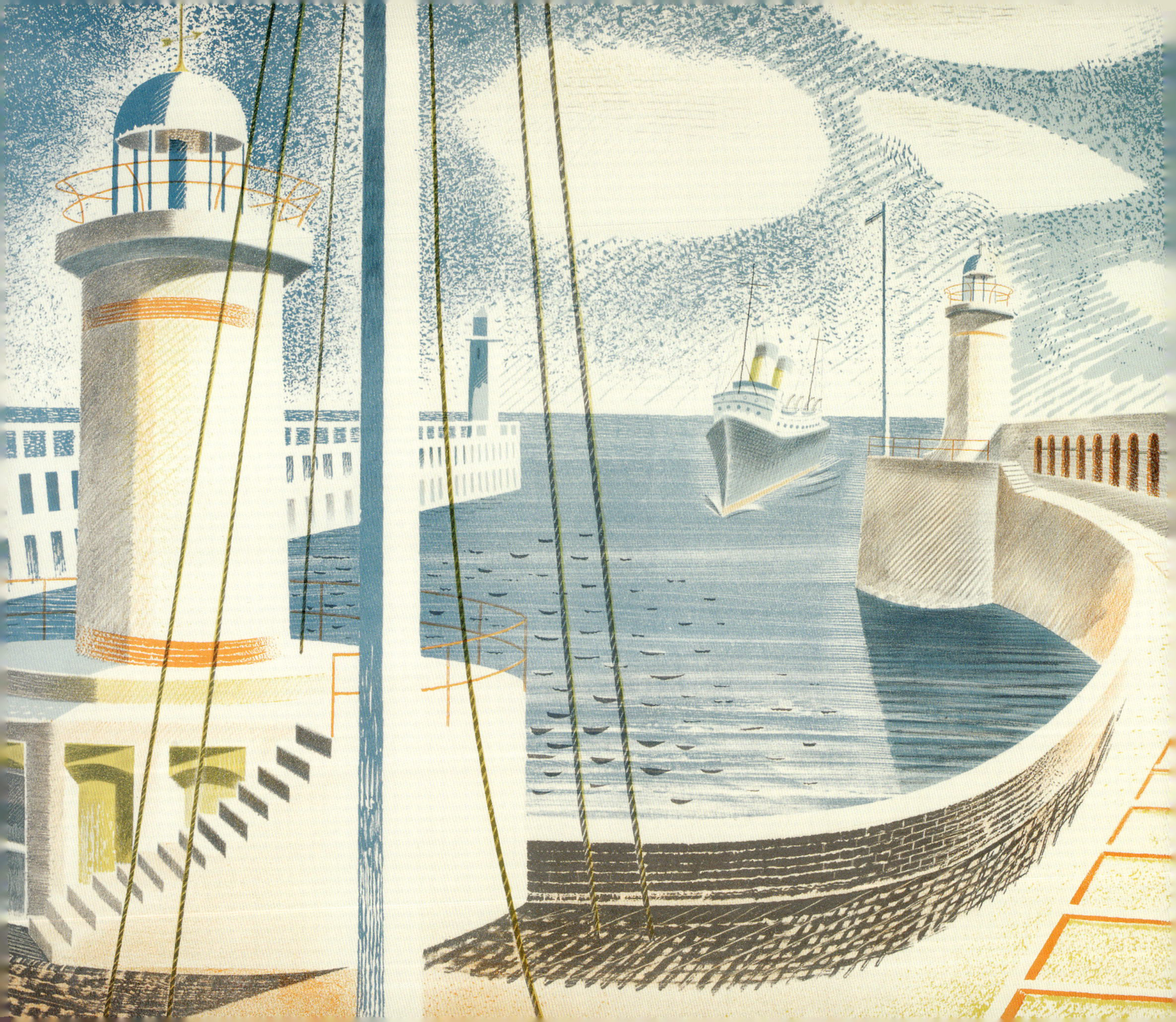

CONTENTS

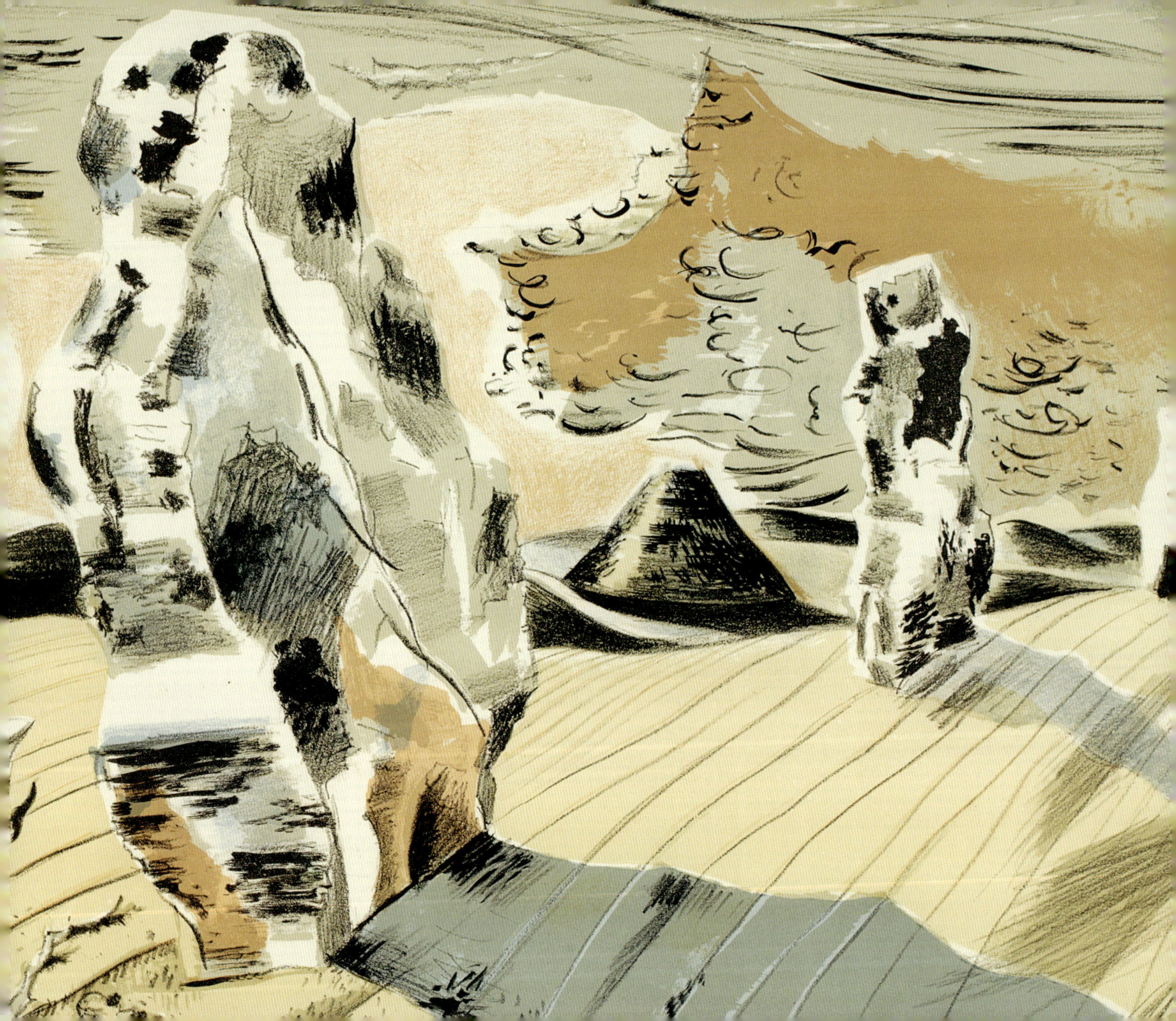

ILLUSTRATIONS

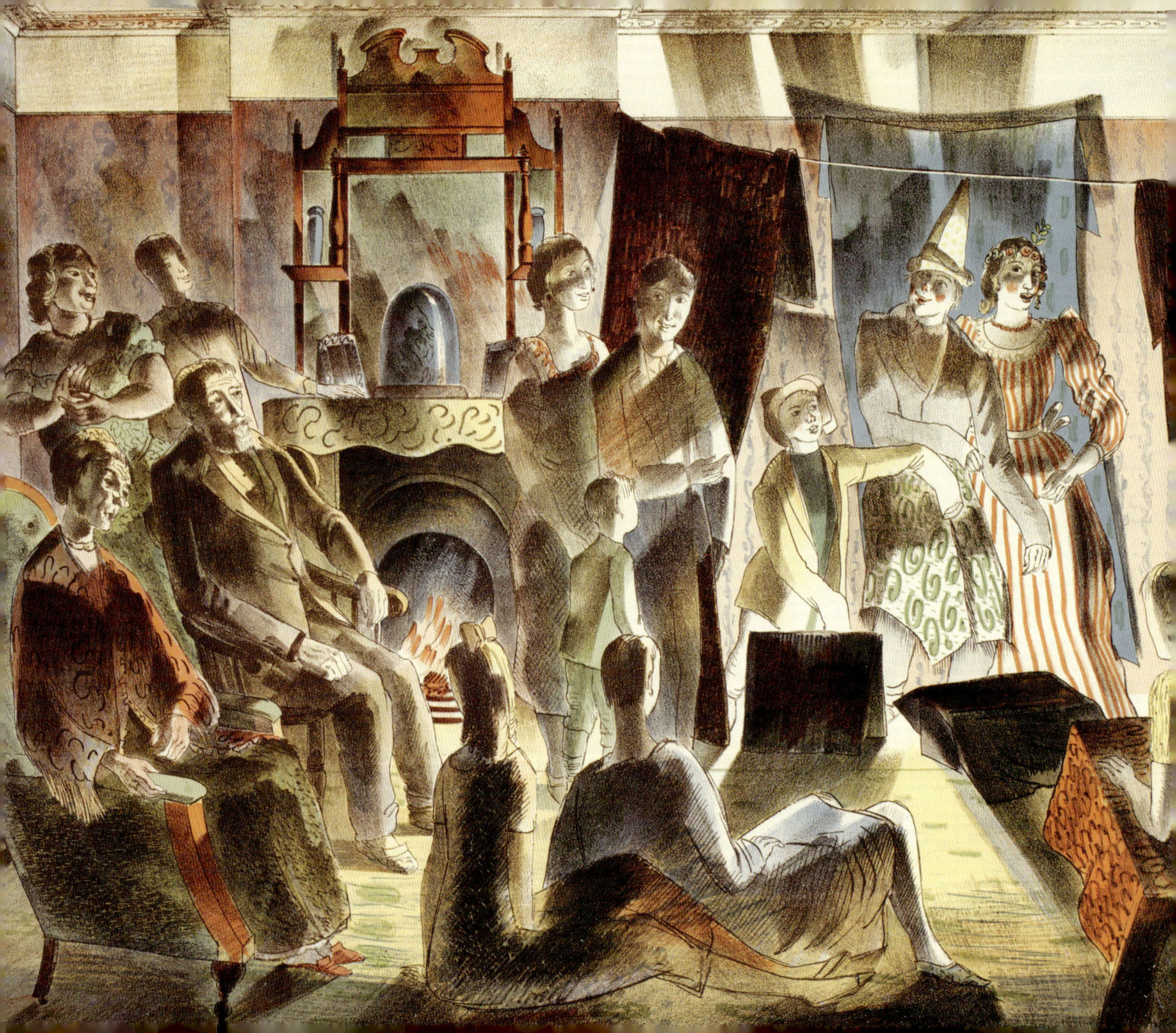

PREFACE

Although probably apocryphal, it is said that Sigmund Freud only needed one example in order to construct a theory. The common herd, with rather more grounded, plodding brains, to whom Eureka experiences are unlikely to occur, work more cynically along the lines that 'one swallow doesn't make a summer'.

Imagine my own delight when I stumbled upon not one, but some half dozen or so examples of commissioned art print series produced in England in the first half of the 20th century. Talking numbers, my prosaic, statistically-trained, brain was relieved to find that each series contained sufficient numbers of items, varying from about twelve to into the fifties; sufficient enough to begin to 'make a summer' for me. Here was a curious phenomenon worth looking at.

From an art history angle it began to interest me as to why some artists had been selected, and others excluded, in the commissioning of each series; what did each group of commissioned artists represent as a sample; could one generalise from each group as to what was going on more broadly on the English art scene at the time; or were the artists some particular clique, some minority group, with a more vague or limited significance?

And beyond such questions lay more psychological and sociological ones – what motivated the commissioners of such series; were there hidden agendas to the more overtly declared ones; to what extent was the commissioning of artists a matter of benevolent patronage for the artists, providing them with necessary funds, or benevolent patronage towards the general population along the lines of 'bringing art to the people'; were the projects energised by propaganda and commercial considerations or were they ego-trips for those involved ?

Certainly the Ministry of Information WWI – 'Efforts and Ideals' – (the first of the series), one which used such quality artists as Frank Brangwyn and C.R.W.Nevinson, although producing some remarkable aesthetic images, was published to gear the people's energies towards winning the war; presumably 'good' art was equated with strong impact. And the company-sponsored series of J.Lyons & Co., in the late forties and early fifties, had primarily been conceived as a practical means of refurbishing their restaurants and cafes in a time of rationing, and only secondly as a public relations exercise associating the name Lyons with 'good' art and thereby 'upping' the firm's image – only as a by-product did it become a 'people's art gallery'. The fact that neither of these print series had as its initial aim the art education of the population in no way detracts from their significance to art historians, particularly to those interested specifically in printmaking.

Even with such series as 'Contemporary Lithographs' (1937-8), the Artists' International Association's 'Everyman Prints' (1940), Brenda Rawnsley's 'The School Prints' (1946-9), the 'Festival of Britain' Series (1951) and the 'Coronation' Series from the Royal College of Art (1953), where the overt aim was to bring good representative art to the people by producing quality prints at reasonable prices, the motivation turns out to be rather more complex than just the altruism of art education.

Contemporary Lithographs Ltd was a company apparently set up to do just that. Just prior to WWII, it commissioned two series of auto-lithographed prints, primarily to be sold to educational institutions, not only to brighten the walls, but to sensitise pupils to really looking at pictures and perhaps, beyond this, to make pictures themselves.

One can look at this simple scheme of 25 images from a variety of angles – it can be seen as a sample of the sort of subjects and styles characteristic of the artists at the time; it can be explored as part of the relatively short-lived revival of auto-lithography as an art medium; its existence can throw light on the network of relationships that existed then, between art colleges, art dealers and commercial printers; and it can be tied into the many, often naïve, 'Utopian' egalitarian schemes of the inter-war years; and so on. Lesser mortals can embroider as complex a sampler from a sufficient number of events as Freud could from one.

I should have started writing about these series in some sort of chronological order but I came across the J.Lyons & Co. series first, when visiting the 'Tea and a Slice of Art' exhibition at the Towner Art Gallery, Eastbourne. The charm of the show brought a wave of nostalgia to me and as a result the Towner was encouraged to produce a book in support of their own collection of Lyons' Lithographs. This motivated me to produce a sister book on The School Prints and now on Contemporary Lithographs. Working backwards like this is not the most illuminating way of tackling the 'series' phenomenon but this is how it came about.

My enthusiasm was such that I was not deterred when coming across a comprehensively researched article written on the subject by Antony Griffiths, now Keeper of Prints and Drawings at the British Museum. My determination not to be thwarted by the fact that an account had been done on Contemporary Lithographs that could hardly be bettered, led me to the rationalisation that it was published some time ago (1991) and in a journal not readily available to the public *Print Quarterly*. I fully acknowledge my debt to Mr. Griffiths, indeed my extensive use of the information in his article; my excuse is my tendency to want to popularise. The facts in this book are largely Mr. Griffith's; the opinions, particularly the more extravagant and eccentric ones, are my own.

A Note on References

I have drawn from the following key texts in most of the chapters:

1977 Pat Gilmour, *Artists at the Curwen*, Tate Gallery

1990 Frances Carey & Antony Griffiths, *Avante-Garde British Printmaking 1914-1960*, British Museum

1991 Antony Griffiths, *Contemporary Lithographs Ltd*, *Print Quarterly Vol. VIII 4*

1992 *British Printmakers 1885-1955*, Garton & Co.

ART FOR EVERYONE

ART FOR EVERYONE

It may be a trifle farfetched to claim any direct link between a modest print scheme in the late 1930s, (aiming to bring 'good' art to education), and the building of Britain's grand public art galleries in the late 19th and early 20th century, yet both are elements in what can be described as the democratisation of art.

Bringing art out of its pampered environment of private houses and palaces into public galleries must certainly be credited as having a popularist base. Yet the municipal buildings, the vehicles for this, seem, in hindsight, more a matter of swagger and parochial competitiveness than of accessibility for the masses; their flights of stairs, titanic pillars, echoing entrance halls and uniformed flunkies were, and still are, deterring, rather than inviting.

And the art within such marble halls seems also to have had a swagger to it – the swagger of local gentry, industrialists, and other *nouveau riche*, declaring their wealth and their artistic discernment. The subject matter of their gifts to the public was equally to impress – Greek mythology, ancient battles, biblical scenes and ancestral portraits – towards which the general public could have felt little, if any, affinity.

As late as 1938 W.E.Williams, who was involved in the Institute of Adult Education's 'Art for the People Scheme' (which had started in 1933) bemoaned the fact that 'In over four hundred towns with a population of over five thousand there aren't any municipal collections of pictures at all to be seen'. Similarly Robert Lyon, writing of his Worker's Education Association art project with the Ashington miners in 1936 wrote of how he was appalled to find that there wasn't even a public library locally and the nearest art gallery was in Newcastle some twenty miles away.

When Eric Newton summarised the position for the British Council in 'Art for Everybody' (1943) he described the contemporary art world, before WWII as being 'so completely concentrated into a couple of square miles of the West End of London that it is no wonder that vast areas of England were, and still are, unfamiliar with the achievements of our contemporary painters'. However, he offered a small ray of hope – '... in our smaller provincial towns the number of travelling art exhibitions is steadily increasing though the supply has by no means caught up with the demand'.

The difference between the grandiosity of the Victorian and Edwardian art galleries and the small projects of bringing good art to the masses, like Contemporary Lithographs, is not so much a matter of size but of ethos. The zeitgeist of the public galleries was one of paternalism, along with such town planning schemes as the Cadbury's laying down for others the right ways of living, in Selly Oak, Birmingham. The intent of the small schemes was more egalitarian, with a greater faith in people's innate desire to learn and respond when the opportunity was given.

That ordinary people had a valid voice and were eager for self-development was not just a matter of extending the electoral roll. Optimism was afoot in Britain in the 20s and 30s, in spite of, or possibly spurred on by, the bleak realities of economic depression and the rise of totalitarianism. Both the birth of the documentary film movement, in the 20s, by the combined efforts of a young social scientist and an imaginative civil servant – John Grierson and Stephen Tallents, and later its tie in with Mass Observation, the social research brainchild of Tom Harrison and Charles Madge, gave ordinary people a kind of vote by validating their lives and their opinions.

Myriads of organisations were springing up, in the inter-war years, based on the faith that if cultural provision was on offer there were sparks to be lit in everyone. The Worker's Education Association and the Institute of Adult Education have been mentioned. And then there were the Village College schemes of Henry Morris (to become an instigator of Contemporary Lithographs Ltd) who saw the need for education provision from birth to old age. Even the Youth Hostels Association can be seen as part of this cultural swirl, helping townies, with their restricted means, to appreciate beauty in the countryside.

The launch of Penguin Books, in 1935, seemed also to be plugging into this zeitgeist of optimistic egalitarianism. Allen Lane set out to produce well-designed paperbacks of worthwhile content and priced at 'no more than a packet of cigarettes'. John Miles described even the Penguin covers, with their two horizontal slabs enclosing the author and title as egalitarian – 'No matter how grand or famous the author the typographic treatment was exactly the same'. Lane was aiming to replace the cheap and garish in other publishers' books that he had seen on station bookstalls, as Robert Wellington and John Piper with their Contemporary Lithographs venture would try to replace poor quality reproductions.

And then there were more blatantly cultural left-wing projects suggesting to the common man and woman that the millennium was just round the corner and that they were central to it – the Left Review (1934), the Artists' International Association (1933), Victor Gollanz's Left Wing Book Club, and their ilk. As James Fitton put it 'Everyone was to the left in those days'.

Where did 'art' stand in this whirl of democratisation? Well 'fine' art appeared to be floating in rather heady country well above the general population. On one hand, there was Unit One (1933) and Ben Nicholson's purging of the 7&5 Society, both moving in the direction of Objective Abstraction/Constructivism with their accompanying exhibitions – Zwemmer's Objective Abstractions (1934), the Mayor Gallery's Unit One show (1934) and Nicolette Gray's 'Abstract and Concrete' at Lefevre(1936) with their associated catalogues and publications, as Myfanwy Evans (Piper)'s *Axis*. On the other hand there were the psychoanalytically inspired Surrealists, prominent, but equally out of touch with the common herd, with their International Surrealist Exhibition at the New Burlington Galleries (1936).

Anthony Blunt was to write scathingly of these two 'fine' art streams in the *Left Review* (April 1937) – 'They have served their purpose in destroying the old standard of capitalist culture, but they have no roots at all in the proletariat, and therefore their contribution cannot lead to the new culture which will come about from the socialist state'. This reads somewhat hollowly in 2007, given Blunt's subsequent royal association.

A more muted stream of British traditional social realism in art was continuing on its way via Sickert and the New English Art Club. None of this work had any particular political drive to it. Coldstream explained his own stance in developing realism with the Euston Road School – 'The Slump had made me aware of social problems, and I became convinced that art ought to be directed to a wider public; whereas all ideas which I had learned to regard as artistically revolutionary ran in the opposite direction. It seemed to me important that the broken communication between the artist and the public should be built up again and that this most probably implied a movement towards realism'.

It was the Artists International Association (AIA) that most actively allied realism in art to left wing politics. Misha Black, one of its founder members described his own attitudes – 'It just arose from the conviction that artists should play a part in society apart from producing works of art, which they sold or didn't sell...' But AIA had more mixed motives than this. James Boswell summed up the mixed bag that was AIA– 'agit-prop body, Marxist discussion group, exhibitions organiser and anti-war, anti-fascist outfit.... conservative in art and radical in politics'.

Whatever its more grandiose declarations of purpose AIA showed a practical concern on the matter of the limited opportunities for people to see contemporary art outside London. As with the Institute of Adult Education they took exhibitions of original art on the road (32,000 were said to have visited one of these when it arrived in Bradford). And eventually AIA arrived at the idea of 'the print' being the cheapest and easiest way of taking 'art to the people' with their Everyman Prints (1940).

Of course fine print making had existed for centuries but it was the efforts of the likes of Campbell Dodgson, at the British Museum, that provided a new impetus to it in the early 20th century. Dodgson not only built up the Museum's collection but encouraged collectors with his editing of *Print Collector's Quarterly* and later editing the annual *Fine Prints of the Year.* And then there were the major commercial art galleries as Colnaghi's, Lefevre, Redfern, St Georges and the Fine Art Society not only selling fine prints but commissioning them. However, all this was for elite groups, with the means to buy or the enthusiasm to search out the British Museum Print Room.

Frances Carey and Antony Griffiths suggest that the roots for the popularisation of art through the print lay in more humble quarters with the flowering of the poster. There had been a limited use of 'fine' artists, by government, to produce posters for propaganda purposes; but it was such entrepreneurial mavericks as Frank Pick at London Transport, Stephen Tallents at the Empire Marketing Board and later the Post Office, and Jack Beddington at Shell, who more fully exploited the poster. All of them had their own organisations' aims to meet – getting more people to use buses and trains, to buy Empire goods, to use Post Office services or to buy more petrol. Yet all three of them, in the 20s and 30s, came under the spell of artists, felt personally enriched by associating with them, and yet cynically realising that to link their organisations to 'fine' art would be gaining 'fine' reputations and thereby greater income.

So art came to the masses not so much through municipal galleries, or even evangelical touring exhibitions, but by billboards, on the sides of passing vehicles and in shop windows. The response of the public to the simple, brightly coloured images of the likes of McKnight Kauffer or Hans Schleger, took the commissioning agents by surprise. Such was public enthusiasm that Frank Pick felt obliged to open a shop at London Transport Headquarters on Broadway where his posters could be bought for a shilling or two. *The Studio* (1933) hyped these as being 'pleasing pictorial posters – pictures to harmonize with your decorations'.

Stephen Tallents, at the Empire Marketing Board (EMB) was overwhelmed by public demand, particularly from schools, for the Board's posters. At first EMB just made surplus stock available to education, but eventually the Board produced special versions of the most popular posters on more robust paper to survive the school usage. By the early 30s EMB was supplying 27,000 schools. Such was the success of this that when Tallents moved to the Post Office in 1933 one of his first projects was to commission artists to produce poster prints in series of threes and fours specifically for schools. These contained no blatant advertising but illustrated aspects of the history of the Post Office and the reach of its activities. Of course Tallents' aim was primarily that of public relations, but nevertheless the result was that, at the very least, school walls were brightened and pupils made aware of how good quality colour prints of interesting subjects compared to the dreary brownish scenes of classical or biblical themes to which they had been previously exposed.

In many instances the distinction between a poster and an artist's print became blurred and often came down to edition size (artists' prints limited to editions of tens or low hundreds, posters being unlimited and produced in thousands), and to whether the print was signed or not. The word 'poster-print' seems to have been coined for prints of poster size with no obvious advertising copy on them.

Such was the climate when two young men, Robert Wellington, still in his 20s, and John Piper, in his early 30s, decided to set up Contemporary Lithographs Ltd in 1935 to commission artists to provide prints for schools. The project was perhaps more directly linked to fine art print distribution (as Wellington was dealing in prints at Zwemmer's art gallery), but also picked up some of the left-wing fervour of 'art for the people' without either participant being strongly politically motivated. The initial target for proselytising fine art prints was that of the Post Office school posters, a market where they would be in competition with the young idealist, Derek Rawnsley, with his School Prints Ltd, hiring fine art reproductions to schools.

Neither Wellington nor Piper appear to have acknowledged any previous scheme as influencing their decision to start out in this direction. And later similar schemes as Brenda Rawnsley's 30 School Prints (1945-9), the AIA Everyman print series or the AIA/School Prints 'Festival of Britain' Series make no reference to Contemporary Lithographs Ltd as inspiring them.

Yet all these schemes, along with the later commercial ones of J.Lyons Ltd (1947-55), Guinness (1956-7), and the series issued by the Royal College of Art (starting with the 'Coronation Series' in

1953) were part of an 'Art for the People' ethos in mid-20th century Britain. It is, perhaps, only with hindsight that such efforts can be linked together not only by their direct or indirect intent, but by the artists involved (many contributing to more than one scheme), by the general content and style of their images (the British scene) and by their medium, lithography.

References

1934 Herbert Read, *Unit One*, Lund Humphries

1938 R.S.Lambert, *Art in England*, Penguin

1963 Ronald Blythe, *The Age of Illusion, England in the Twenties and Thirties 1919-1940*, Penguin

1979 Christian Barman, *The Man Who Built London Transport, a biography of Frank Pick*, David & Charles

1980 *Thirties, British art & design before the war* Arts Council/V&A

1983 Lynda Morris & Robert Radford, *AIA, the story of the Artists International Association 1933-53*

1984 catal. *Unit One: spirit of the 30s*, The Mayor Gallery

1986 Frances Spalding, *British Art since 1900*, Thames & Hudson

1986 Stephen Constantine, *Buy and Build, the advertising posters of the Empire Marketing Board*, H.M.S.O.

1987 Robert Radford, *Art for a Purpose, the Artists' International Association 1933-1953*, Winchester School of Art Press

1987 ed. Susan Compton, *British Art in the 20th Century*, Royal Academy

2004 Peyton Skipwith, *Britain between the Wars 1918-1939* Fine Art Society

2006 Ruth Artmonsky, *Jack Beddington, the footnote man* Artmonsky Arts

THE PERSONALITIES

THE PERSONALITIES

Apart from the commissioned artists. five people, each remarkable characters in their own field of work, were to be involved in the Contemporary Lithograph project. The sole directors throughout the life of Contemporary Lithographs Ltd were Robert Wellington, a precocious young art dealer, managing the avant garde Zwemmer's Art Gallery in London, and John Piper, at the time (along with his wife-to-be Myfanwy Evans), championing abstract art in Britain. The educational input came from Henry Morris, then pioneering the 'village college/education for life' concept in Cambridgeshire. The book designer/typographer Oliver Simon, and the master printer, Harold Curwen, were to ensure the highest standard of commercial print-making for the enterprise, whilst furthering the cause of auto-lithography, particularly dear to Curwen's heart.

ROBERT WELLINGTON, ART DEALER (1910-1990)

It seems remarkable that a teenager, with few academic or vocational qualifications, and no relevant experience, should have been given the responsibility of running one of the most influential London art galleries, but that is what happened to Robert Wellington when, in 1929, he went to Zwemmer's Art Gallery at 26 Litchfield Street, off the Charing Cross Road.

Young Wellington had probably acquired some useful French and German from his short spells at Montpelier and Freiburg universities and by living with a painter's family in Munich; this would have been a strong point in his favour for a gallery that was intent on having a European outlook.

And if later personality strengths, as described by Robert Medley in his obituary of Wellington, were beginning to show – 'sophistication, with a critical judgement that was warm-hearted and instinctive...ambitious, driven by a strong ego...' they would also have been a plus. But still, a smattering of languages, charm and drive don't seem entirely adequate qualities to account for his selection.

The missing factor would seem to lie in Wellington's family background. For his father, Hubert was a key figure in the London art world at that time. Hubert Wellington was, himself, an artist, and although Robert Medley is rather dismissive about his talents – 'a lesser-known artist of the Camden Town, Spencer Gore group' – Hubert's work was bought by the Tate and the Arts Council.

With a young family to support Hubert turned to teaching and writing, both of which brought him to the attention of William Rothenstein, the newly appointed Principal of the Royal College of Art. In particular Rothenstein would have been drawn to Hubert's monograph of Rothenstein (1923) and would have found intriguing Hubert's pioneering of guided lectures at the National Gallery, his reviews in *The Nation*, the *Manchester Guardian* and the *Saturday Review*, along with his books on Epstein and Delacroix.

In no time Hubert was appointed Rothenstein's 'chief of staff' at the College. In *Men and Memories* Rothenstein records his gratitude to Hubert – '(he) took from my shoulders much of the administration, and through his insight and sympathy in his dealing with students and staff, brought an inspiring energy to the service of the college, a new spirit pervaded the students'. Piper, a student at the college in 1926, recalls how he scraped into the Painting School through the kindness of Hubert Wellington. Wellington was later to become Principal of the Edinburgh College of Art (1932 - 1942) where he appears to have created a similar atmosphere of goodwill, setting out to make his student 'good Europeans'.

The Wellington family were living in Downshire Hill, Hampstead, in the late 20s. Young Wellington grew up in a home where he was likely to be having tea with the Gilmans or 'at homes' with the Epsteins. Downshire Hill, in the 20s and 30s, was to be the home, for varying periods, of the Carlines (Richard and Hilda – Mrs. Stanley Spencer), Roland Penrose and Lee Miller, and of the bookman, Oliver Simon. The nearby roads were saturated with artists and art critics – Herbert Read, C.R.W.Nevison, Ben Nicholson, Barbara Hepworth, David Bomberg, Mark Gertler, and, to become Contemporary Lithographers, Ivon Hitchens and Paul Nash. Art must have come to Robert Wellington by osmosis, by pollution!

Further factors of relevance, albeit indirectly, were that Robert's grandfather had a large printing firm in the City, and his father, Hubert, whilst still studying at the Slade, was encouraged to an interest in prints and printmaking by Lawrence Binyon, at the British Museum print room. Printing was in the background, if not in the genes.

In spite of Wellington's possible youthful sophistication/charm/social networking, his actual appointment to Zwemmer's was achieved by the personal intervention of the family neighbour and William Rothenstein's nephew, Oliver Simon. It was Simon who alerted Robert to the fact that Anton Zwemmer was looking for someone to run his new gallery; and who recommended Robert to Zwemmer. It was then up to Robert to prove himself

Ann Baer, who was to be involved in selling the Contemporary Lithographs during and after the war, described Wellington's appointment to run Zwemmer's art gallery as normal practice at the time. She remembered a manager in the Ministry of Food, which was being evacuated to Wales, hand-picking interesting, non-civil service people, irrespective of relevant qualifications (of which she, as an art student was typical) so that he wouldn't be bored!

Zwemmer, a Dutchman, had purchased, by 1923, a bookshop on the Charing Cross Road. Zwemmer gradually built up his stock to become the principal source of art books and periodicals in London. In addition he began to sell high quality reproduction prints imported from such reputable print publishers as the Marees Society and Piper Verlag of Munich. Campbell Dodgson, the Director of the Print Room at the British Museum, described many of these prints as technically perfect. Zwemmer, himself, seems to have had at least a thread of social-mindedness in selling prints as he advertised them as providing 'the man of moderate means with his only opportunity of indulging on his own walls his millionaire taste for the real thing, otherwise only to be gratified by visits to rare exhibitions'.

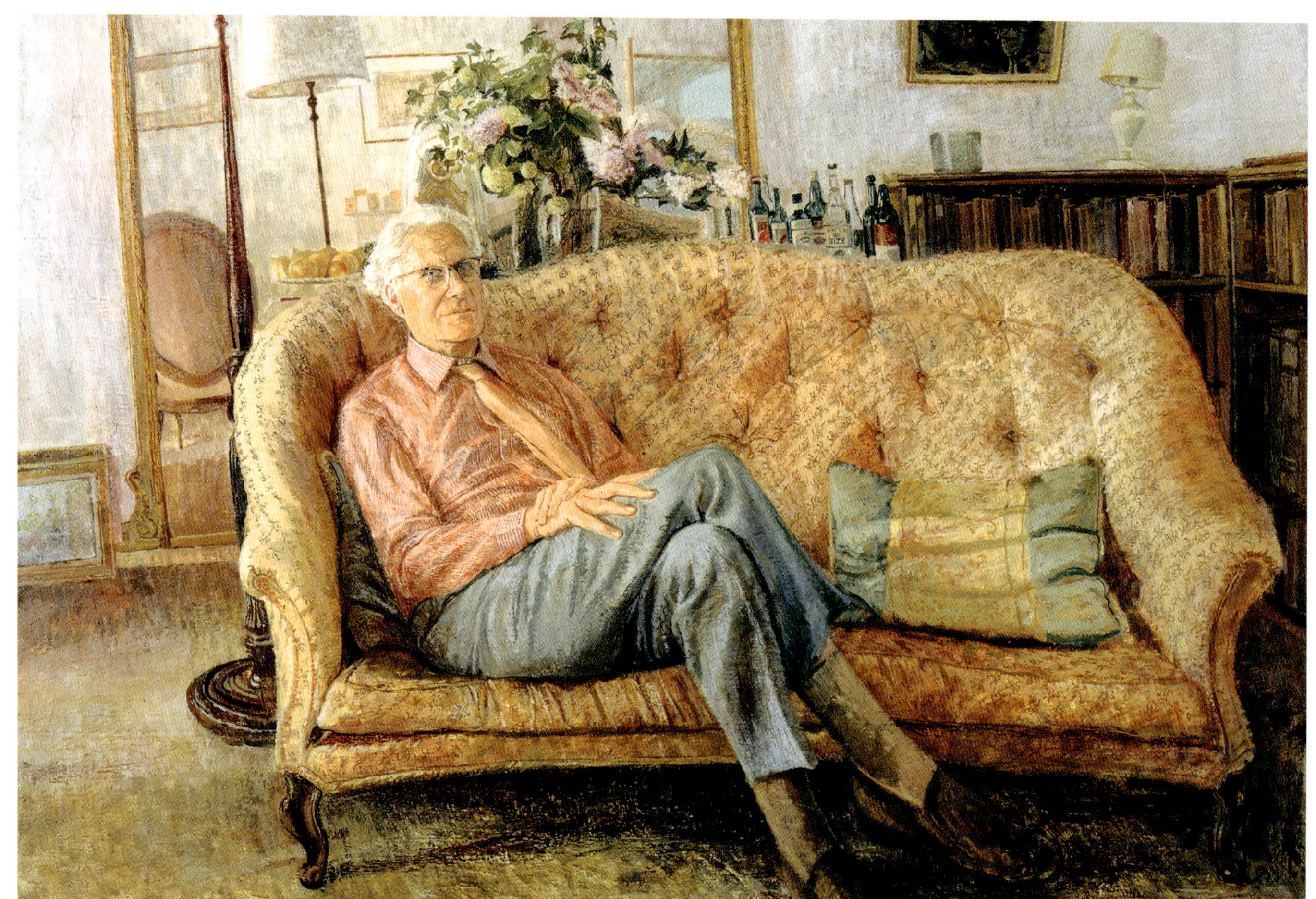

Portrait of Robert Wellington by Maurice Sheppard (Cardiff Museum Art Gallery)

Could this 'missionary' element to sales have been contagious for the young Wellington?

By 1929 Zwemmer's enthusiasm for contemporary European prints was such that he decided to open an art gallery across from the bookshop and it was here that Wellington was to serve his apprenticeship. His conditions of service were that he would be paid a basic salary and a commission on sales. He was allowed a nearly complete autonomy to plan and mount what exhibitions he would as long as he worked around Zwemmer's own exhibitions of Europeans such as Dali and Picasso (the only selling show to be put on of his works in the United Kingdom in the 1930s).

Wellington's original remit was to sell first class reproductions but it did not take him long to build up his own coterie of artists from his father's students at the Royal College. The first sign of Robert taking 'ownership', as it were, was his exhibition of contemporary artists in 1930 with a repeat of the same artists in 1933, many of whom would be used in the Contemporary Lithographs. Amongst the artists Wellington was to show were Victor Pasmore, John Piper, Barnett Freedman, William Coldstream, Rodrigo Moynihan, Ceri Richards, Ivon Hitchens, Graham Sutherland, Frances Hodgkins, Barbara Hepworth, David Jones, Robert Medley and Edward Wadsworth. He gave solo exhibitions to Norah McGuiness (1934), to Edward Bawden (1933) and to Eric Ravilious (1933). The likes of Wyndham Lewis were critical of Wellington for his exclusiveness, presumably, in Lewis's case, because he was amongst the excluded.

In 1932 Wellington became the first business manager of Group

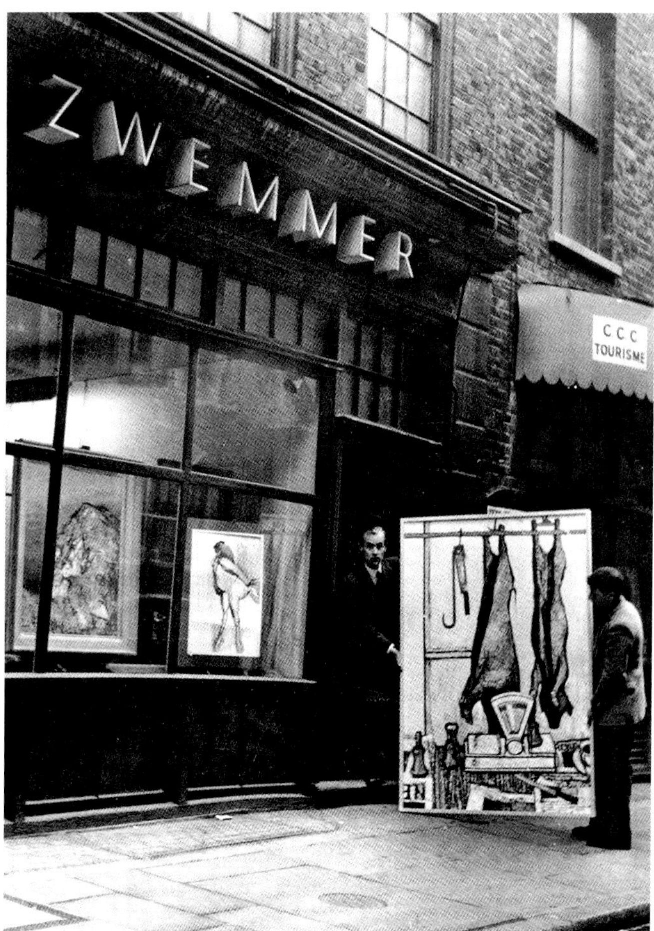

Zwemmer's Art Gallery, Litchfield Street

Theatre, an experimental group started by Robert Medley's partner Rupert Donne. Although this was not politically active, as was the Unity Theatre, its *raison d'etre* was for all involved – artists, technicians, designers, and authors – to be equal members of a creative team, and to have the audience democratically involved as part of each project; as Auden put it 'every member of the audience should feel like an understudy'. Medley described him as lively, perceptive, and energetic, but not excessively businesslike. This all seems prophetic of Wellington's contribution to Contemporary Lithographs Ltd – enthusiastic, idealistic but not really commercially effective.

That Wellington's motivation was not entirely commercial or ego-driven was perhaps seen in his scheme for a 'Centre of Contemporary Art' conceived in 1934. This seems to have consisted of providing a guaranteed income to a select group of artists along with a declared number of exhibitions; something along the lines of Maynard Keynes and Samuel Courtauld's scheme in 1925. Roy de Maistre, who had good connections, helped Wellington draw up a memorandum outlining the idea. Henry Moore said he could give up teaching and concentrate on his work if guaranteed £400 a year. However Wellington failed to raise the necessary capital and the scheme foundered. Nevertheless here, perhaps, were the seeds of his concern for 'his' artists, to surface again in Contemporary Lithographs Ltd.

JOHN PIPER, PAINTER AND PRINT MAKER (1903-1992)

John Piper was something of a late starter and perhaps it was his eagerness to catch up that made the 1930s for him a period of experiment and inner conflict both artistically and personally.

Born into a professional family, his father was a solicitor, Piper was unfortunate enough to have an elder brother killed in WWI. Apart from the personal distress, this led the family ambitions to be laid on Piper's shoulders. His father insisted that he take articles. Accounts differ as to whether his father cut him out of the will because of his artistic ambitions or merely insisted that articles should be completed first. Whichever, Piper was 'set free' by his father's death in 1927; his mother supported him with a modest allowance and eventually, in 1935, was to buy him Fawley Bottom, near Henley, which was to become Piper's lifetime home.

Piper studied at Richmond and Kingston Schools of Art before going to the Royal College (1926-29).

As a boy he had shown a precocious interest in things antiquarian. By the age of fourteen he was said to have visited every church in Surrey; and by fifteen had become the secretary of the Epsom branch of the Surrey Archaeological Society. Here lay the roots that were to be dormant during his 1930s adventures into the abstract but which were to dominate his work from the 1940s.

Piper had early on been something of an experimenter working with wood engravings even before he went to art school. His 1930s experiments came with his exposure to European artists, with Ben Nicholson's influence, and with his meeting with Myfanwy Evans (who was to be come his second wife).

As early as 1927 Piper had met up with Braque (at Jim Ede's house in Hampstead), but it was not until he saw, and was overwhelmed by, the Miro exhibition at Galeries Cahiers d'Art in 1934 that he became drawn to less representational art. And it was about this time that Ben Nicholson contacted him, having been struck by a Piper review of a Wadsworth exhibition. Nicholson got Piper elected to the 7&5 exhibiting society, which Nicholson was then purging of its representational work. Piper seems to have been more than mildly attracted to what the Society was about for he quickly became its secretary, and chairman of its hanging committee. He was to have six works in the Society's last exhibition at the Zwemmer Gallery in 1935, producing his first abstract works. Piper was later to write of his membership – 'It taught me something of the value of clear colours, one against another, when they have no goods to deliver except themselves'.

And it was about this time – 1934- that Piper was introduced to Myfanwy Evans, who had been acting as a model for Ivon Hitchens. Myfanwy, an English graduate just down from Oxford, was full of enthusiasm for what was happening in the art world. With introductions from Piper, she met up with Helion in Paris and, through him, visited Mondrian, Brancusi, Kandinsky and Giacometti. She came to the conclusion that these wonderful artists needed their own voice and a shop window to display their wares. She returned to England determined to start a journal which would argue for abstractionism. *Axis* was born.

Piper was quickly drawn into the project as general assistant, article writer and illustrator, and seems to have provided a home for the journal as *Axis* was largely produced at Fawley Bottom. The first issue appeared in January 1935 subtitled 'A Quarterly Review of Contemporary 'Abstract' Painting and Sculpture'. *Axis*, in its issues seems to have been grappling with the same aesthetic conflicts as Piper himself. Starting off wholely devoted to abstraction it began to falter, particularly in relation to Surrealism.

In 1936 Piper was writing that he hoped abstract painting would become 'lucid and popular and not in the least bit highbrow'. And in his article 'England's Climate', in *Axis's* seventh issue in 1936, he appeared to be declaring war on both abstraction and realism. In *The Painter's Object*, a book edited by Myfanwy in 1937, Piper showed the direction of his thinking – 'it will be a good thing to get back to the tree in the field.'

Myfanwy, herself, seemed also to be backtracking, for in her introductory article she wrote 'We have got into not one but a thousand battles. Left, right, black, red (and white too, for the fools who won't take part and so contribute a battle line all of their own), Hampstead, Bloomsbury, surrealism, abstract, social realist, Spain, Germany, Heaven, Hell, Paradise, Chaos, light, dark, round, square'. *Axis's* 8th and final issue came out in winter 1937.

It may be far-fetched to see as symbolic of Piper's inner struggles, at that time of the production of Contemporary Lithographs, the fact that during WWII he offered the safety of Fawley Bottom to both the library of the Society of Antiquaries as well as to the records of the radical Group Theatre (for whom, incidentally, Robert Medley, a Contemporary Lithographer had been the chief designer). Fraser-Jenkins describes Piper's conflict between his commitment to the modern and his love of the past as at its most intense in 1937.

Neither Griffiths, in his comprehensive article on Contemporary Lithographs, nor any of the various Piper commentators make mention of the circumstances of Piper's first meeting with Wellington. Piper had been buying at Zwemmer's bookshop from the beginning of the 1930s, remembering a 1931 edition of Cahiers d'Art as having 'a profound and lasting collection of influences on me'. Halliday, in his history of Zwemmer's, suggests that the 7&5 Society may have chosen to exhibit at the Zwemmer Gallery in 1935 actually because of the Piper's contact with Wellington. This may have been part of the general swirl of young artists gathering there, of which Piper would have been one; but more specifically they would have met when Piper was visiting to negotiate Zwemmer's distribution of *Axis*, towards the end of 1934 or at the beginning of 1935 and there is also the possibility they overlapped with the Group Theatre with which Piper was to to make his debut as a stage designer. Whatever the circumstances of their meeting, the mutual attraction and respect of Wellington and Piper must have been sufficiently strong for them to start out on their joint venture, The Contemporary Lithographs Ltd

HENRY MORRIS, EDUCATIONALIST (1889-1961)

Henry Morris abhorred the wasted life. He had used his own life fully, starting from modest beginnings (his father had been a plumber), and he saw education as the means of helping people develop their potential, not just when they were young, but as an ongoing process

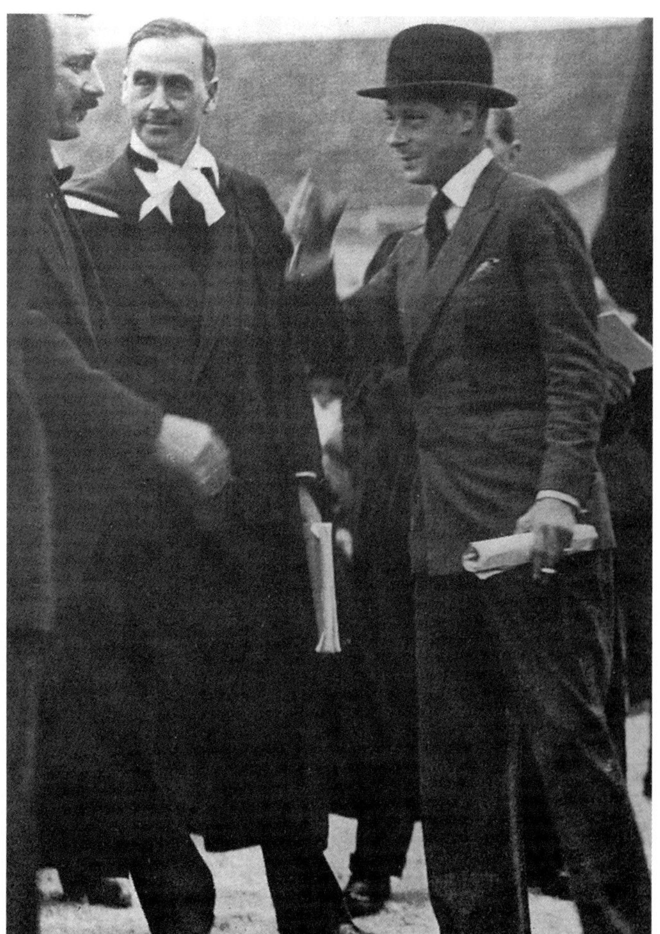

Henry Morris (centre) with the Prince of Wales, 1930

of enrichment from birth to death. He was not only to transform rural education but was to revolutionise school architecture and design.

Morris, himself, left school early aged 14, and began work on a local paper – *The Southport Visitor*. His ambitions turned towards the church and he went from studies at the Harris Institute in Preston to St David's, Lampeter, taking a degree in theology. He went on to Exeter College, Oxford, but his studies were interrupted by WWI in which he was commissioned in the Royal Army Service Corps.

Here were the two strands that were to contribute to his effectiveness in the education world – a religious-like evangelism for his particular cause, and a military-like approach to planning and implementation – focussed and cunning. At the end of the war he transferred to King's College, Cambridge to complete Part I of a Moral Sciences Tripos.

He decided his cause, and battlefield, would be education. On leaving Cambridge he started work in the Kent Education Offices but within a couple of years he had joined Cambridgeshire where he was promoted to County Education Secretary (equivalent to Chief Education Officer) at the precocious age of 33. He was to work in that position for some 32 years leaving his mark not only within the county but nationwide.

In Cambridgeshire Morris inherited a depressed rural economy with the resultant decay of communities inevitably accompanied by inadequate schools, poorly funded. Morris's vision was an education system for the whole community, for all ages, for all aspects of life, and one relevant to rural living – the Village College. The concept is encapsulated in his writings and speech making – 'It is the life the adult will lead, the working philosophy by which he will live, the politics of the community which he will serve in his maturity, that should be the main concern of education.

In practical terms this meant that education should be related to need (be practical rather than theoretical); that the school or college should merge with the community and not be isolated; and that it should be concerned with the mind, the body and the soul rather than merely with the absorption of facts – that a school or college should be a workshop for living.

The idea was revolutionary, uplifting and optimistic. And Morris's strength, in moving quickly from the drawing board to the site, was his cleverness at playing the system. He was a maverick from within rather than an outside challenger. By 1927 he had got approval for the first Village College; and 1930 saw him accompanying the Prince of Wales at the opening of Sawston. Colleges at Linton, Bottisham and Impington all opened in the 30s and Bassingham and Gaminglay after the war.

'Art' was central to Morris's concept of 'education for all' for he saw the importance of the effect of the aesthetics of the environment on behaviour. He himself was a fastidious man who lived in some style, whether in his Regency house in Cambridge or in his retirement rooms in Welwyn Garden City.

For Morris, the whole school or college environment should be a considered aesthetic experience, from the architecture of the building to the art and artefacts found in it, to the colour of the walls. His mission has been described as 'encouraging people of all ages using all possible means to the consumption and production of art'.

He broke ground as far as school architecture was concerned, by getting the temporary refugee, Walter Gropius, to collaborate with Maxwell Fry on the building of his Impington Village College. Jack Pritchard, the furniture manufacturer and founder of Lawn Road Flats, (who had been instrumental in getting Gropius, amongst many other intellectuals, out of Germany), wrote of the meeting of Morris and Gropius – 'Enlightened architect met enlightened educationalist; result orgasm!'

And Morris involved another 'passing through' refugee, the Bauhaus designer Moholy-Nagy, with the colour scheme at Linton. Colour was of particular concern to Morris; he could be found on site of any new college surrounded by pots of paints, trying them out on the plaster. He maintained that 'gay and exhilarating colours do not cost more than County Council Brown or Municipal Green'. Single-handedly Morris can be assessed as having led the way in making British educational architecture in the thirties of international importance.

Morris was very concerned to use contemporary architects, designers and artists in his schemes. And he himself would bring back pictures and pieces of sculpture from his various travels and 'lend' them to schools. He would collect works of art and then, personally, place them with loving care in full view of all using the buildings. He saw original works of art not only as decorative, but as actually stimulating creativity in the viewer.

Morris is thought to have met Robert Wellington in Cambridge but the circumstances are not recorded. Wellington merely records meeting Morris 'in the late 20s'. Morris came to visit the Zwemmer Gallery regularly, not only from his own interests, but to acquire works for his schools and colleges. Wellington reported Morris rushing up to London from Cambridge to return laden with piles of reproductions of Impressionists to cover the walls of Sawston for the arrival of the Prince of Wales (1930). This hardly makes Morris out to be a Modernist sympathiser but certainly suggests that he knew what would work for the people on the ground. Yet even into the 30s a Degas dancer or Monet haystack in one's sitting room was considered quite advanced. Wellington can be seen as refining Morris's aesthetic horizons by introducing him to the many young painters visiting and showing at Zwemmer's and gradually Morris began to purchase more modern and original works e.g. those of Ivon Hitchens.

It was Morris's evangelistic energy and optimism, besides his purse, that were to encourage Wellington in his Contemporary Lithographs escapade.

OLIVER SIMON AND HAROLD CURWEN AT THE CURWEN PRESS

Oliver Simon and Harold Curwen have been described as opposites bound together in an assault on ugliness and in a common desire to make printing into an applied art. Curwen was the technical man born and bred, never happier than working with his hands on the shop floor of his Plaistow printing works, concerning himself with general com-

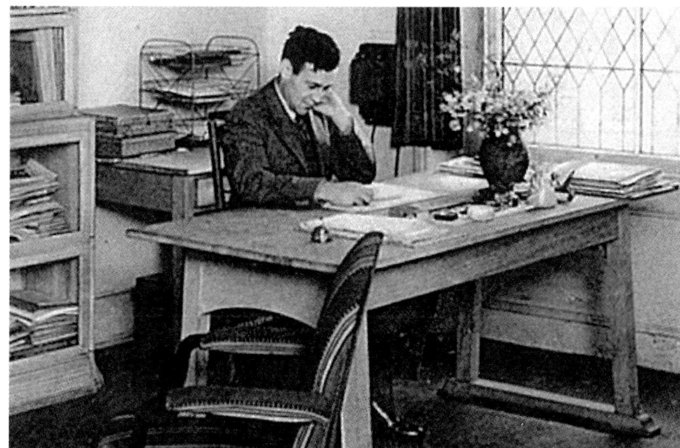

Oliver Simon in his office, Great Russell Street

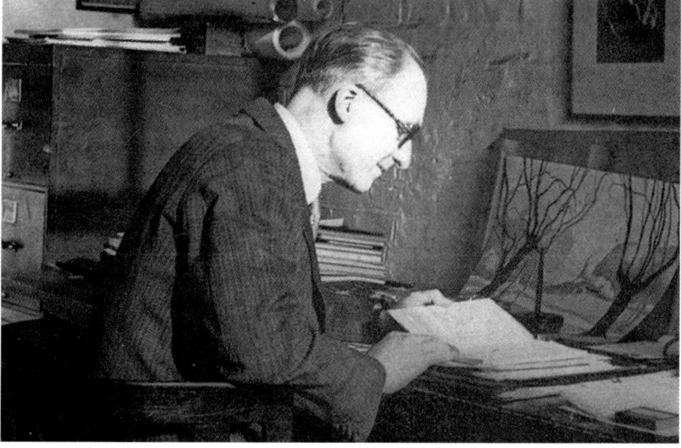

Harold Curwen in his office, Curwen works, Plaistow

mercial printing. Simon had his own empire in the Curwen office in Bloomsbury, which became something like a club where artists and publishers could mix and talk book publishing and design. Curwen was imbued with humanity; he had a genuine concern for the welfare of his 'team' and this was met with a great loyalty and with long term service from his employees. Simon, on the other hand, was very much in charge of his arena, and design decisions were very firmly his. Pat Gilmour wryly wrote of the two 'Oliver Simon could never adjust to a committee of more than one.' Yet the two together, later with Simon's brother Herbert, were to set the standard for fine printing throughout the mid-20th century.

Harold Curwen (1885-1949) chose to work in the family printing works started by his grandfather the Reverend John Curwen. His preference for being on the shop floor was additionally fostered by his education at the progressive school, Abbotsholme, which stressed that education of the hand had an equal importance to education of the brain. His school was also to imbue Curwen with the democratic values that were to form his management style, for it emphasised, in all its activities, teamwork over competition. As early as 1919 Curwen was to write 'The aim of service to the community leads to better results both productively and socially than does the aim of industrial gain'.

When Curwen started with the family firm, just after WWI he found what he considered 'a visual wilderness'. From the very start he was determined to raise the aesthetic standards of what was being produced at the works. He had started his printing 'apprenticeship' at Abbotsholme, before shop floor training at the Works and a period studying in Leipzig. Additionally he took himself off to Edward Johnstone's typography classes at Central School of Arts and Crafts and very soon began to draw artists into the Works.

Curwen had been a founder member of the Design and Industries Association and through this he met Claude Lovat Fraser in 1919. Very soon Curwen was commissioning a whole variety of work from Fraser – printer's ornaments, posters, booklets, letterheads and similar commercial material. The Curwen publicity began to link higher standards of design with likely sales results along the lines 'Get the Spirit of Joy into your printed things' and 'It's a great pleasure to arrange fine type and still finer artistry to convey the spirit of your message. And work that is pleasurable is usually a success'. Curwen's own publicity repeated the theme – 'It's good fun to do good work, and it also happens to be good business'. It must have been the first time words like 'spirit', 'joy' and 'fun' had ever been applied to jobbing printing!

Haldane Macfall, Lovat's biographer exemplified Curwen's understanding and sympathy with artists when he recorded that 'instead of dragging Lovat down to commercial standards, he brought commercial tracts up to Lovat's, who adapted his picturesque and gay art to it all'.

Everything written about Curwen suggests that he loved having artists about the place and was never happier than when discovering and commissioning new talent. He encouraged his artists to visit the Plaistow works, even when they were not working on their own pictures there, rather than to be one step removed, working through publishers. Of course Curwen is best remembered for his championing of autolithography, but if his artists didn't want to work directly onto stones or plates he would help them to design with a particular print process in mind. His concern was that artists should understand and work cooperatively with his printers, and vice versa; each should respect the competence of the other and recognise their inter-dependence. Curwen was one of only a handful of owners who were able to cut through union prejudice and defensiveness, on the one hand, and artists' sensitivity to the reproduction of their work, on the other, to achieve a degree of mutual empathy.

Harold Curwen got the best out of his work people, as out of his artists, by listening, by consulting and by involving. Any major changes at the Works were balloted; job satisfaction was central to its operations. Curwen was respected, indeed loved by his employees not only for his personality and management style but for his technical know-how – there was not a job Curwen couldn't do as well, if not better, than them.

Edward Bawden recalled, with charm, his start at working with Curwen: 'I went down to the press one day a week as a student, which I thought was thrilling and Harold Curwen, who looked a bit like a scoutmaster, loved explaining how things were done. So I got in among the litho sweats – the men who worked on the litho stones. I did a lot of tiddly jobs for Curwen. He'd say, "Oh come down and we'll do a jam label" – but he'd spend the time explaining how this or that was done'.

Christian Barman ended an appreciation of Curwen with – 'the breadth and catholicity of a mind that could accept and absorb not only the incandescent novelty of artists like Lovat Fraser and the young McKnight Kauffer, but a typographic genius like Oliver Simon with an outlook almost dramatically opposed to his own'.

In 1934 Curwen wrote *Processes of Graphic Reproduction* summarising his ideas on, and experience with, printing.

When Contemporary Lithographs Ltd decided on Curwen as the printers for their scheme Harold Curwen was well-positioned and only too ready to open his doors to them, and to their artists, and able to respond actively and effectively to their requirements. Oliver Simon (1895-1956) was from a background of comfort and culture. His father was a successful Lancashire cotton merchant and his uncles major figures in their respective art fields – William Rothenstein, to become Principal of the Royal College of Art, and Albert Rutherston, illustrator and Principal of the Ruskin College of Drawing. And given that Simon was to become a kind of missionary in his own field of book production, it is of interest that his own parents were enthusiastic members of the Ancoats Brotherhood, founded to carry 'the love of art and beauty to the mean streets of Manchester'.

Simon was an ailing child, with an interrupted education, finally being sent to a boarding school in Germany, where his father had relations. He went on to serve as an officer, in WWI, in the 53rd (Welsh) Divisional Cyclist Company. At demobilisation, he found himself, aged 24, with no particular career in mind.

Simon tells the story of his 'Eureka' moment, on seeing William Morris's Kelmscott Chaucer in Sotheran's window; beautiful books were to become his 'cause'. His brother Herbert described him as becoming an eminent typographer before typography had become a profession. He enrolled in evening classes at Camberwell School of Arts and Crafts, and worked for a short time at Griggs, (a Peckham lithographers); but it was when Simon's uncle Rutherston introduced him to Claude Lovat Fraser who in turn introduced him to Joseph Thorp, an associate of Harold Curwen's, that Simon's real apprenticeship started.

Simon's energy and enthusiasm was such that soon he was taken on by Curwen to try to develop a book printing side for the press. At first Simon shared an office in Westminster with the printman Stanley Morrison; but later he moved to what was to become the Curwen's town office, at 101 Great Russell Street, which was soon a kind of club for those interested in fine publishing and printing, many of those meeting there already with established reputations – Frances Meynell, Stanley Morrison, Holbrook Jackson and Bernard Newdigate amongst them – a set that Simon described as his 'private printing university'.

Simon spread his enthusiasm by starting specialist journals for typography, fine printing and the graphic arts – *The Fleuron* (launched in 1923 and transferred to the Cambridge University Press in 1929 – debts cleared by Simon's father) and later the altogether more successful *Signature* (1935-1954 with a wartime break from 1940-1946 – 33 issues in all). *Signature* was very much Simon's own baby and, over the years he attracted his own circle to write and illustrate for it. Simon was to include, in *Signature*, articles by Barnett Freedman, Paul

Nash, Graham Sutherland, John Piper, Lynton Lamb and Edward Ardizzone, along with articles on Eric Ravilious and Edward Bawden – all to be contributors to Contemporary Lithographs.

Simon's other vehicle for evangelism was to start, with Hubert Foss, a dining club for lovers of the art of the book – the Double Crown Club. The Club held its first meeting on 31st October 1924 and is still active today. Simon guarded the interest of the Club for many years, and was to 'resign' from time to time, when he felt the membership was becoming too commercial, veering too much towards advertising and away from 'the book'. Each dinner was accompanied by a specially designed menu, and a speaker. Again, as with *Signature* many of the artists involved in Contemporary Lithographs were to produce menus for Simon – Bawden, Sutherland, Ardizzone, Paul Nash, Freedman, Ravilious, Lamb, Piper, and Simon himself (for October 1935). Stanley Morison described Simon's contribution to the Club – 'he never did most of the talking, but usually most of the inspiring'.

Although Curwen had already begun to use artists to make his printing more eye-catching, it was Simon who was to open the floodgates of the Works. In this, he was particularly helped by his uncle, William Rothenstein, and soon both students and staff from the Royal College of Art were tripping out to Plaistow. Edward Bawden was still a student when he was given an introduction to Simon at the Great Russell Street office, and so started his long association with the Curwen Press from as early as 1925. Barnett Freedman, in particular, was favoured at the works for his egalitarian 'hands-on' approach. Simon found Graham Sutherland especially important to him, in broadening his education in the arts; (Curwen was to print the *International Surrealist Bulletin* with which Sutherland was associated).

Herbert Simon wrote of his brother that 'he was so nearly an artist who had not learnt to draw, but determined somehow to express himself'; and of Simon and Curwen together – 'They both knew when to enlist the help of an artist and their choice of an artist was rarely at fault'. Desmond Flower of Cassells described Simon's standards - 'he had almost raised his sights to a point at which he could no longer see the sordid earth'. Ann Baer, whose father Frank Sidgwick (founder of the publishers Sidgwick and Jackson) had been in with Simon at the start of the Double Crown Club, considers Simon as having been at the forefront of book design at the time, respected by artists, publishers and printers alike.

Simon, a neighbour of Wellington's in Downshire Hill, and by 1933 a Director of Curwen, was to be pivotal in the Contemporary Lithographs enterprise, bringing his own coterie of artists and his own enthusiasm to the scheme.

For just a few years, prior to WWII, the paths of these five enthusiasts overlapped for the Contemporary Lithographs Ltd enterprise – Wellington from his base as an art print dealer and with his concern to give his artists greater exposure; Piper wrestling with his own demons of traditionalism versus modernism; Morris evangelical for art as central to personal development and education for life; and Curwen and Simon campaigning for aesthetic printing, irrespective of whether the end product was a humble handbill, a book, or an artist's print.

Bibliography

Robert Wellington

1971 Exhibition catalogue, 'Hampstead in the 30s' Camden Arts Centre

1990 10th August Obituary in *The Times* Robert Medley

1991 Nigel Vaux Halliday, *More Than a Bookshop, Zwemmer's and art in the 20th century*, Philip Wilson

2004 William Coldstream, *Wellington, Hubert Lindsay (1879-1967)*, rev.Adrian Lindsay Oxford Dictionary of National Biography

John Piper

1979 Anthony West, *John Piper*, Secker & Warburg

1983 Exhibition catalogue, 'John Piper', Tate Gallery

1987 Orde Levinson, *John Piper, the complete graphic works, a catalogue raisonne 1923-1983*, Faber & Faber

2003 David Fraser Jenkins/Frances Spalding, *John Piper in the 30s, abstraction on the Beach*, Dulwich Picture Gallery

Henry Morris

1965 Norman Fisher, *The Arthur Mellows Memorial Lecture – Henry Morris, pioneer of education in the countryside*

1973 Harry Ree, *Educator Extraordinary, the life and achievement of Henry Morris 1889-1961*, Longmans

1998 Tony Jeff, *Henry Morris: Village College, Community Education and the Ideal Order*, The Educational Heretics Press

Oliver Simon and Harold Curwen

1923 Haldane Macfall, *The Book of Lovat*, Dent & Sons

1951 Oliver Simon, *To The Fleuron*, Signature No.13

1956 Christian Barman, *Harold Curwen*, Penrose Annual vol.50

1956 Oliver Simon, *Printer and Playground, an autobiography*, Faber & Faber

1957 Herbert Simon, *A Note on Oliver Simon*, The Penrose Annual vol.51

1973 Herbert Simon, *Song and Words, a history of the Curwen Press*, George Allen & Unwin

1974 James Moran, *The Double Crown Club, a history of fifty years*, Westerham Press

1977 Pat Gilmour, *Artists at Curwen*, Tate Gallery

THE NETWORK IN MID 1930s

Hampstead Neighbours
Robert Wellington, Oliver Simon, Ivon Hitchens, Paul Nash

Royal College of Art
William Rothenstein – Principal
Hubert Wellington – Registrar
One-time students
Edward Bawden, Raymond Coxon
Barnett Freedman, Vincent Lines, John Piper
Eric Ravilious, Randolph Schwabe
One-time teachers
Edward Bawden, Barnett Freedman, John Nash
Paul Nash, Eric Ravilious, Randolph Schwabe

The Curwen Press
Harold Curwen & Oliver Simon – Directors
Curwen Artists
Edward Bawden, Barnett Freedman, John Nash
Paul Nash, Eric Ravilious, Graham Sutherland
Signature
Oliver Simon – owner
Contributors
Barnett Freedman, Paul Nash, John Piper,
Lynton Lamb, Edward Ardizzone

Zwemmer's Art Gallery
Robert Wellington – Manager
Exhibiting artists
Edward Bawden, Barnett Freedman, Ivon Hitchens,
Frances Hodgkins, Norah McGuiness, Robert Medley
Paul Nash, Eric Ravilious and Edward Wadsworth

THE START-UP

THE START-UP

There seems to be no clear account as to who originated the idea of commissioning artists to do auto-lithographs for schools. Robert Wellington certainly took the leading role. He might possibly have already had an embryonic idea from hearing about Simon's uncle, Charles Rutherston, who had left his art collection to Manchester, to be loaned out to schools. However the trigger for the project largely arose from his dealings with Henry Morris and his belief that an aesthetic educational environment would better pupil's development. The venture would also have drawn encouragement from the 1935 report of the Council for Art and Industry on Art in Elementary and Secondary School Education which included the opinion 'that children's surroundings, and the first impressions created in their minds, are important factors influencing their development and their outlook on life...The whole course in Art should aim at enriching the stock of images which the child gathers at school. Out of a liberal store will come efforts at comparison, and out of efforts at comparison will come attempts at criticism'.

Morris's opinions, along with the then current educational thinking and 'art for the people' zeitgeist, all had their influence, reading between the lines of Wellington and Piper's prospectus for the scheme (undated but apparently published after the issue of the first 10 prints as it contains press reviews) –

> 'An increasing number of teachers feel that it is essential that schools should have some original works of art on their walls, and not only machine-made reproductions. Only the wealthy schools can hope to afford oil or water-colour paintings. We have kept in mind the importance of providing pictures costing not more than one pound each, which is within the means of every school and makes changes in the scheme of decoration possible';

and further –

> We should like to discourage the feeling that good pictures are exclusively museum objects: things which were no longer produced after 1800 or 1900, and which have no connection for children with their personal discoveries in chalks and paint or with such present-day paintings as may come their way'.

Roger Berthoud, in his biography of Graham Sutherland gives Sutherland remembering Morris as being the 'original stimulant' for the scheme. Morris's frequent demands on Zwemmer for prints for his schools and colleges led Wellington to suggest to him that it would be even better if he could involve living artists in his schemes. It is known that a variety of possibilities were mooted – a mural by Robert Medley and a fountain by Henry Moore, being two. Morris was said to have so excited Moore by his concept of the community and the family being at the core of his village colleges that Moore started on his

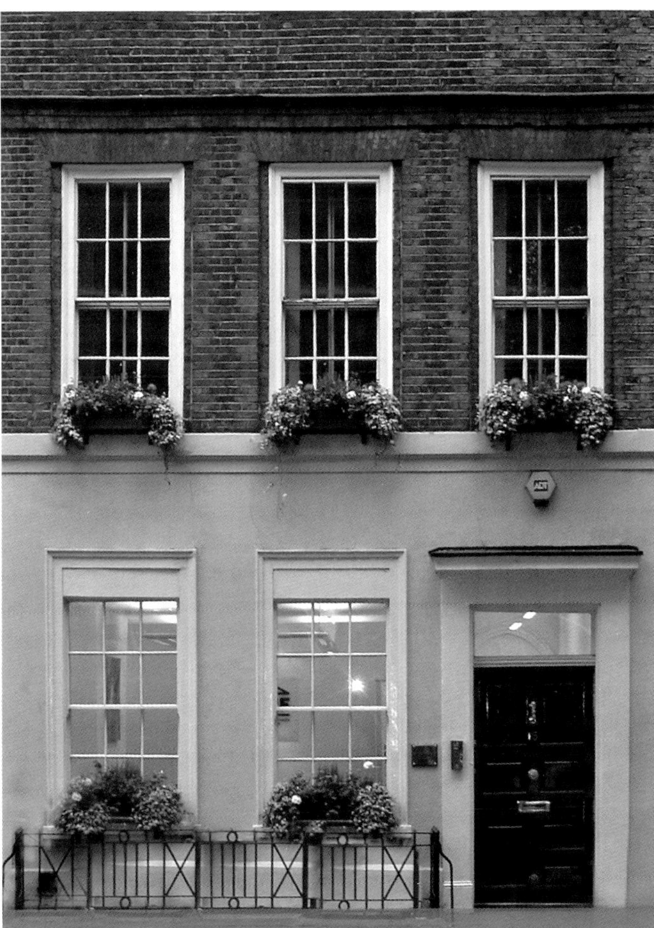

Contemporary Lithographs Ltd offices, Soho Square

CONTEMPORARY LITHOGRAPHS LTD

Directors:
ROBERT M. WELLINGTON
JOHN PIPER

15 SOHO SQUARE
LONDON, W.1
GERRARD 1159

November 4, 1936

Barnett Freedman, Esq.,
11 Canning Place,
W. 8.

Dear Freedman,

I should like to confirm our approval of your drawing of a charade for the lithograph which you are drawing on the stone for us, and which I looked at with you the other evening.

The terms which we propose are a payment of twenty pounds within ten days of our receiving delivery of the prints. The edition will be limited to 420 copies, of which 400 will be for sale. We propose a further payment in royalties of one shilling per print on the first two hundred sold, and two shillings per print on the second two hundred sold, making a possible total payment of fifty pounds in all.

The area of the colour surface to be shown of the lithographs is 20" x 30"

Of the twenty copies not for sale, five are the property of the artist.

Yours sincerely,

For CONTEMPORARY LITHOGRAPHS, Ltd.,

Robert M. Wellington.

Director.

I enjoyed Monday evening so much. What attractive people the Applebaums are — and what a Scot, Grierson!

Wellington's letter to Barnett Freedman confirming his inclusion in the scheme

'family group' studies. (Moore was later to give Morris a maquette of one of his groups). At this stage the art-educationalist, Marion Richardson, was also drawn into their discussions on the matter of getting artists to paint murals.

However, all of this proved too much for Cambridgeshire County Council who, on financial, and possibly on aesthetic, grounds, refused a budget. It seems to be, when rebuffed by the local authority, that Wellington came up with the idea of producing limited-edition auto-lithographs for schools; an altogether more economic scheme. Morris thoroughly supported the proposal. Henry Ree, Morris's biographer, confirms this – 'Typically he (Morris) by his new found enthusiasm resulted in action for he was instrumental, through encouragement and financial backing in getting Robert Wellington with John Piper to found Contemporary Lithographs Ltd in 1935'. Nigel Vaux Halliday, in his history of Zwemmer's also states 'Morris was also personally to be a backer for Wellington's joint venture with John Piper.'

Piper is not referred to in relation to the first discussions between Wellington and Morris. Pat Gilmour describes his assigned role as 'to act as works manager at the Curwen Press for those artists who were new to the process (auto-lithography) and wanted help'. Piper was to describe the venture as run by himself, Robert Wellington and Oliver Simon. Wellington recalls considering Piper an asset, not only because of his experimental artistic skills but because of the family's possible financial support.

That Simon, and therefore the Curwen Press, were involved

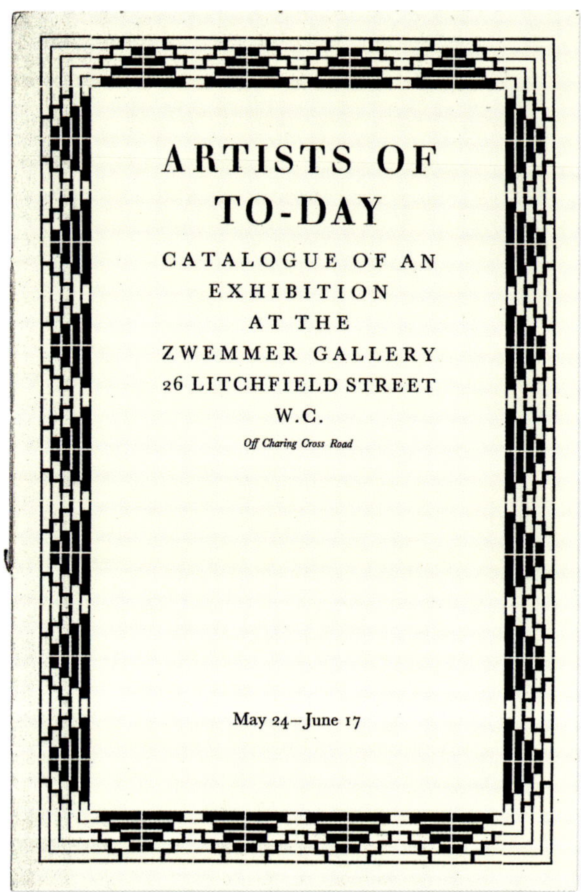

A Zwemmer's catalogue for one of Wellington's 'young artists' exhibitions, printed by Curwen Press

from an early stage was from a convolution of relationships – Simon being a neighbour and friend of Wellington's, both their relations – Simon's uncle and Wellington's father 'running' the Royal College of Art, the Curwen Press having a history of work for Zwemmer's and providing work for many young Royal College students, and so on.

That Curwens was chosen as printers was not merely because of an old-boy network. Two factors would have been crucial to the choice. Wellington and Piper had settled on auto-lithography as the print medium; by then Harold Curwen was one of the two leading printers with a near-religious fervour for advancing the cause of autolithography (the other being Thomas Griffits at the Baynard Press). Additionally, Curwen's sympathetic understanding of artists, of directly involving artists, and of frequently providing open access for them at the Plaistow works, would have argued for Curwen being printers to the scheme.

The scheme was then to commission 'original' prints, produced by contemporary artists, and sold at a modest price. The 'originality' of the prints may further have been hyped by Wellington and Piper declaring that only four hundred copies of each would be printed ie implying limited editions. Yet instead of underlining this they put forward the curious argument that by limiting numbers 'any one subject shall not become tiresome by over-repetition' – as if any school would buy more than one copy of any image. The argument for 'originality' will be revisited when the effectiveness of the scheme is evaluated.

That the pair were anxious as to how the schools would actually display their prints was covered by their offering 'suitable mounts and frames at a price as reasonable as that of the lithographs themselves'. Their rather stuffy concern (and perhaps concern for sales) led them to add, in the prospectus, 'The framing of a picture may make or mar it from a decorative point of view'.

Halliday dates Wellington's leaving Zwemmer's as around the end of 1935; work on the series had begun by 1936. In hindsight the pair's naïve optimism led them to take expensive offices on the second floor of a Queen Anne house at 15 Soho Square, where a secretary was installed and orders processed. Besides a secretary they had the part-time help of one, Ormerod Greenwood, a founder member of the Group Theatre to which both Wellington and Piper were connected. And again, underlining Morris as an *éminence grise* to the scheme, they took on Harry Ree (who had been Morris's assistant) for the first sales tour of the country, presumably because someone in the company needed to have had first hand experience of schools.

Much of this account is gleaned from later recorded memories of some of those involved. There were no minutes of meetings or archives of correspondence; that was not Wellington's style. He and Piper were two young men, eager to get going, unhampered by formality.

Without records one can only make presumptions as to how Contemporary Lithograph Ltd artists were selected. They seem mainly to have been drawn from the tangled web of relationships between Hampstead dwellers, the Royal College of Arts students and teachers, Wellington's Zwemmer clique, and the Curwen artists. Piper had fellow students at the RCA, his personal friends and his *Axis* artists to draw upon. Simon, of course, also had his uncle's contacts to use as well as artists contributing to *Signature* and his 'book' artists, many of whom had been nurtured by Curwen at The Works. The same names pop up repeatedly from Hampstead, Kensington, Bloomsbury and Plaistow.

Paul Nash is a typical case. Although not a Royal College alumni, he was to teach there for short periods and William Rothenstein had taken a personal interest in Nash's artistic development; he was a Hampstead dweller, alongside Wellington; he showed at Zwemmer's from appearing in their first exhibition of work from the Curwen Press (1930) and mounted his own exhibition there – 'Room and Book' (1932); Nash had met Simon in the early 20s and was working with the Curwen from 1925; everybody knew everybody.

Wellington and Piper in their publicity, presumably to give gravitas to their scheme, claimed that most of the artists involved were in some way connected with schools of art. In that all their artists had studied either on a full- or on a part-time basis at an art school, apart from John Aldridge and John Nash, this was fairly obvious a fact. Bawden, Freedman, Ravilious and Coxon had all been students at RCA in the immediate post-WWI, brilliant entry; Piper and Lines being there in the late 20s.

Piper and Wellington could further claim to have netted lecturers as well as students; Lynton Lamb was an instructor in Book Production at Central School of Arts and Crafts, Coxon had taught Piper at the Richmond School of Art, Medley and Sutherland were teaching at Chelsea, and Bawden, Freedman, Ravilious and Schwabe were all teaching, at least for short periods, at the Royal College, having studied there.

And then the educational icing on the top for Contemporary Lithographs Ltd, was their getting four college principals to agree to take part – Schwabe at the Slade, Vincent Lines at Hastings, Williamson at Chelsea and Gardiner at Goldsmiths.

Many of the Contemporary Lithographs artists were also in the Zwemmer Art Gallery and Curwen stables. Bawden had his first solo exhibition at Zwemmer's in 1933, with another in 1936; Ravilious's first solo show with Zwemmer's was such a success that Wellington decided to hold his work permanently in stock; Freedman, too, had his first exhibition at Zwemmer's when they showed his illustrations for *Memoirs of an Infantry Officer* (1931). Wellington's mixed shows – 'Artists To-day' (1930 & 1933) included Hitchens, Hodgkins, Medley, Norah McGuiness, Wadsworth and Paul Nash. Piper had shown in the last 7&5 society show held there in 1935. Wellington met, and gave support to Sutherland from about 1932.

In addition to Paul Nash, Bawden, Freedman, John Nash, Ravilious, Ardizzone and Sutherland had all worked with Harold Curwen for the Press prior to Contemporary Lithographs Ltd. Oliver Simon recorded his first meeting with the diffident Bawden, who had an introduction from Harold Stabler, one of his RCA tutors.

'He laid his portfolio of drawings before me on my table and I examined them with great interest. When I had finished I looked up, prepared to make some appreciative comments, only to find that Bawden had already picked up his portfolio and was silently withdrawing, backwards from the room. Infected by his shyness I opened the door for him and, still without a word, the visit was over'.

Bawden worked for Curwen from 1926 when he started by producing some wallpaper designs. He became a personal friend of Harold Curwen and was writing to him for lithographic advice even after Curwen had retired. Freedman's lively activities at Plaistow have been well recorded in Ian Rogerson's book on Freedman's graphic works.

Simon had made use of some of the Curwen Press artists for his early editions of *Signature*. Graham Sutherland, whom Wellington had introduced to Simon described him as 'of immeasurable help to me in every possibly way, encouraging me to write and reproduce my work in *Signature*.

I have not found any formal contracts between Contemporary Lithographs Ltd and the artists commissioned, and, has been said, Wellington was not prone to formality. However, a letter to Barnett Freedman in 1936 seems roughly to cover the conditions of the commissions. It appears that the artists were invited to submit a preliminary sketch. If this were approved, the terms offered were that 420 copies of the auto-lithographed work would be made of which 400 would be for sale, five would be the property of the artist and presumably the remaining fifteen would be the property of Wellington and Piper to distribute as they would. The royalty arrangements were one shilling per print on the first two hundred sold, and two shillings per print on the second two hundred sold. Wellington pointed out to Freedman that the total sum each artist could therefore expect would be £50.

Ten artists were commissioned for the first series issued in 1937; thirteen for the second (Piper producing 3 lithographs) issued in 1938.

Bibliography
Undated prospectus, *Lithographs for Schools*, Contemporary Lithographs Ltd

CONTEMPORARY LITHOGRAPHS

Series One (January 1937)

1. *Cattle Market*, Edward Bawden
2. *Charade*, Barnett Freedman
3. *Buckinghamshire Farm*, Clive Gardiner
4. *Fisherman's Beach*, Norah McGuiness
5. *In the Park*, Robert Medley
6. *The Stour near Bures*, John Nash
7. *Landscape of the Megaliths*, Paul Nash
8. *Newhaven Harbour*, Eric Ravilious
9. *The Sick Duck*, Graham Sutherland
10. *Bears at Tea*, H.S.Williamson

SERIES ONE

1. *CATTLE MARKET*, EDWARD BAWDEN (1903-1989)

Edward Bawden was born in Essex and spent most of his life there. Whilst still at school he attended Cambridge Municipal School of Art (from 1919 on a fulltime basis). He won a scholarship to the Royal College of Art in the design school. Even as a student Bawden chose to be versatile being influenced by his tutor, Paul Nash, to know no boundaries. Whilst at the RCA he took classes at The Central School in book binding and engraving (he was to become the foremost lino-cutter of his time).

From the time he was a student Bawden was doing work for Curwen, along with commissions from London Underground. Soon after leaving college he began his long association with Fortnum & Mason, Shell-Mex (some 30 commissions) and Faber & Faber (from 1932 with the *Good Food* series). He was the quintessential 'jobbing' artist and only to be admired for that.

In WWII he was appointed an Official War Artist working in Europe, the Middle East and Africa.

After the war he continued providing his characteristic images – simple lines, flat colours, touched with whimsical, sometimes wry humour – for book illustrations, advertising and publicity along with murals and decorative work. Parallel to his commercial work he was a prolific water-colourist.

Bawden received an OBE (1946), became a Tate Gallery Trustee (1951) and in 1956 an RA. In 1989 the Victoria & Albert Museum held a retrospective for him, and the Fine Art Society mounted a centenary exhibition (2003).

Bawden's Contemporary Lithograph was actually a transferred linocut (see page 96). It is of Braintree Market near his home in Great Bardfield. Pat Gilmour wrote of the lithograph – 'Happy cows...a Bawden speciality... (it) encapsulates the scene at Braintree cattle-market, incorporating grass-churning yokels and the bland faces or angular haunches of serried ranks of the livestock waiting to be sold'. It was Bawden's only pre-war editioned print.

Collections

Cecil Higgins Art Gallery (contents of studio), Imperial War Museum, V&A, The Fry Art Gallery (Saffron Walden)

References

2005 Malcolm Yorke, *The Inward Laugh*, *Edward Bawden and his circle*, The Fleece Press

2005 Jeremy Greenwood (intro.Elspeth Moncrieff), *Edward Bawden*, *exhibited prints*, The Wood Lea Press

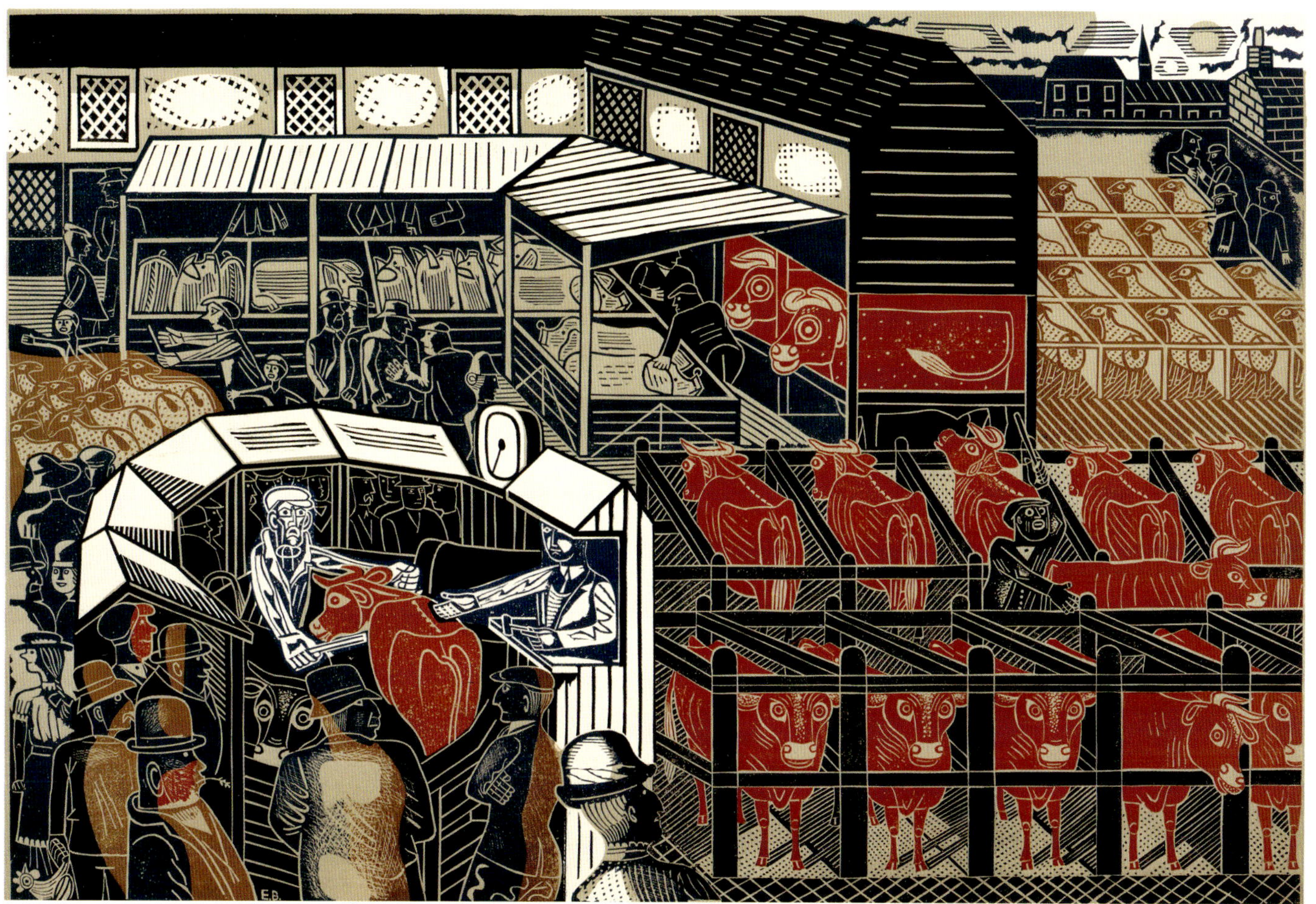

2. *CHARADE*. BARNETT FREEDMAN (1901-1958)

Barnett Freedman was born in Stepney of Russian-Jewish immigrant parents. He attended evening classes at St Martins whilst doing a number of menial jobs. On his third attempt he gained an LCC scholarship to RCA, with the assistance of William Rothenstein.

Freedman became a major book artist – (covers, illustrations, end pieces). His first commission was for Siegfried Sassoon's *Memoirs of an Infantry Officer* for Faber & Faber (1931) for which Zwemmer's gave a show of the illustrations. Freedman worked on over 80 publications, mainly for Faber & Faber, but also for Collins, and the American Limited Editions Club and Heritage Press.

In the 30s Freedman did posters and other publicity material for Jack Beddington at Shell. He became a leading 'jobbing' artist providing advertising material, greetings cards, packaging, stationery, and other ephemera for firms. He did work for the Post Office for some sixteen years, including the 1935 Jubilee stamp.

Freedman taught at the Ruskin School of Art (1929-49) and at RCA from 1930, becoming an honorary fellow. The Arts Council mounted an exhibition of his work (1958).

Initiated by Thomas Griffits, Freedman was the foremost exponent of auto-lithography. He started working with Harold Curwen in the early 30s and most of his book works were printed at Plaistow.

Freedman's Contemporary Lithograph is reminiscent of the many Christmas cards he produced showing convivial social scenes. These were usually small vignettes which he has worked up into a full-blown party for his lithograph. His total command of the medium comes across in his subtle colour combinations with the play of the firelight.

Collections

Freedman's archives are in The Special Collections, Manchester Metropolitan University

References

1948 Jonathan Mayne, *Barnett Freedman*, Art & Technics

2006 Ian Rogerson, *Barnett Freedman, the graphic work*, The Fleece Press

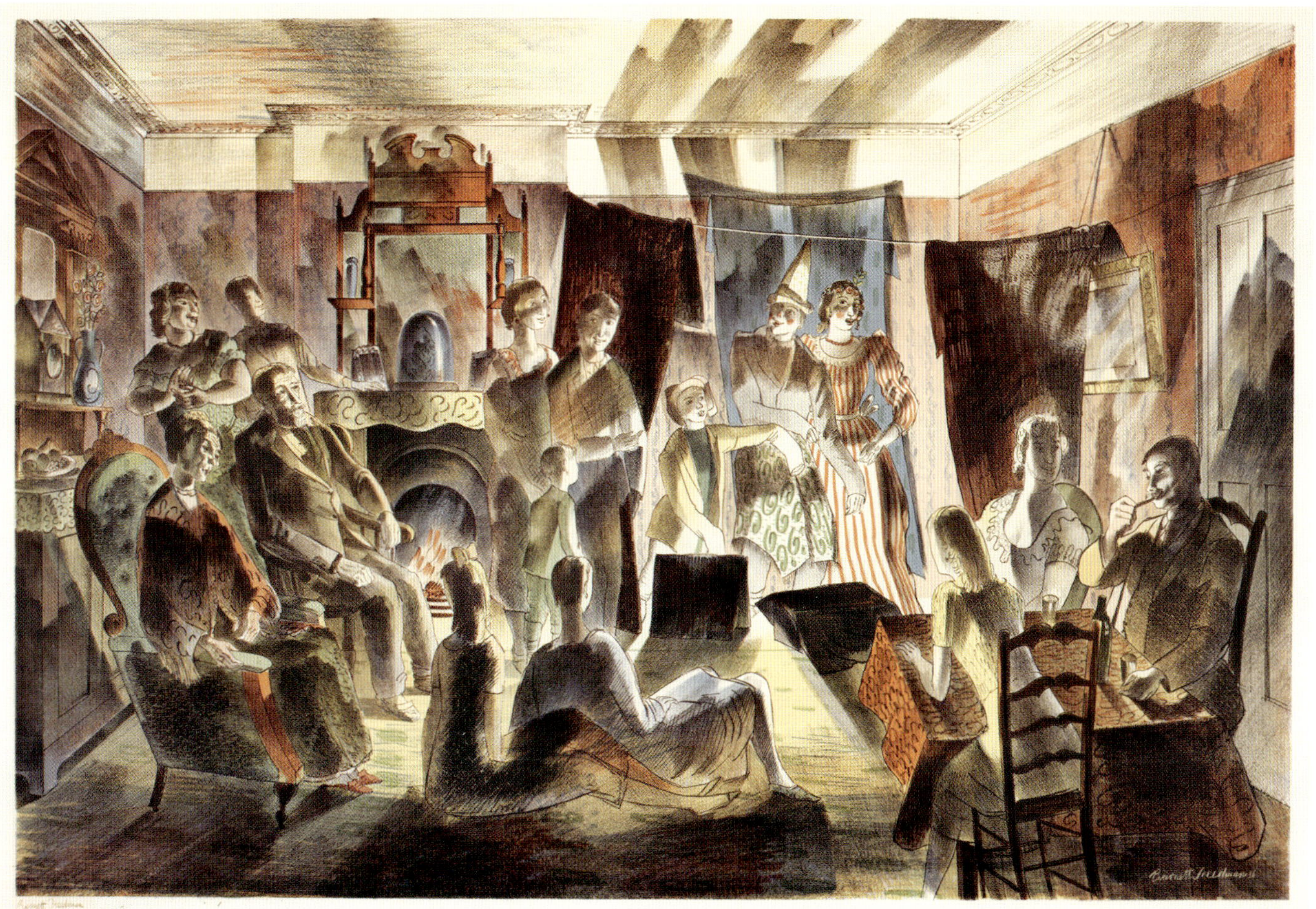

3. *BUCKINGHAMSHIRE FARM*, CLIVE GARDINER (1891-1960)

Clive Gardiner was born in Blackburn, Lancashire but brought up in Great Missenden, Buckinghamshire where he became friends with two young neighbours, John and Paul Nash. Gardiner went to the Slade from 1909 to 1912 and then spent a year at the Royal Academy Schools.

During WWI he worked with the Ministry of Munitions, but immediately after the war he began on what was to become a most distinguished teaching career. For a time he taught at Brighton School of Art and, on a part-time basis, at Bolt Court. In 1929 he became Headmaster, later termed Principal of Goldsmith's College of Art, and he remained there until he retired in 1958. He was remembered by many who came under his influence as inspirational and much loved; he did a good deal for the reputation of the College.

John Lewis, the book designer, said of Gardiner that he 'made Goldsmith's a very happy place'. Lewis recalled of his days there, that Cézanne was the only artist who mattered to Gardiner, and that his teaching was full of 'significant forms'.

Prior to WWII Gardiner was a major poster designer of 'modernist' tendencies. The posters of factories that he did for Stephen Tallents, at the Empire Marketing Board, in the 1920s are outstanding. Gardiner was to do work for all the big poster commissioners of the time – such as London Transport and Shell-Mex. His poster of the *Palm House* at Kew Gardens for London Transport (1926) has become iconic. His stylistic, rhythmic images, were considered revolutionary. His reputation matched that of McKnight Kauffer or Frank Newbould.

Gardiner also did some book illustration, and further, as was popular at the time, he produced murals – for London University and Toynbee Hall, and, during WWII for the British Restaurants. Memorial shows of his work were mounted by the Arts Council (1963) and by the South London Art Gallery (1967).

Gardiner's Contemporary Lithograph of a Buckinghamshire Farm although attractive in its simplicity and in its evocation of the mythical tranquillity of English ruralness, shows nothing of the brilliance and adventurousness of his early poster work; presumably the farm was near where he was living, but it is not identified.

References

1955 Dorothy Dymond, *The Forge; the history of Goldsmith's College*, Methuen

1991 Anthony E.Firth, *Goldsmith's College: a Centenary Account*, Athlone Press

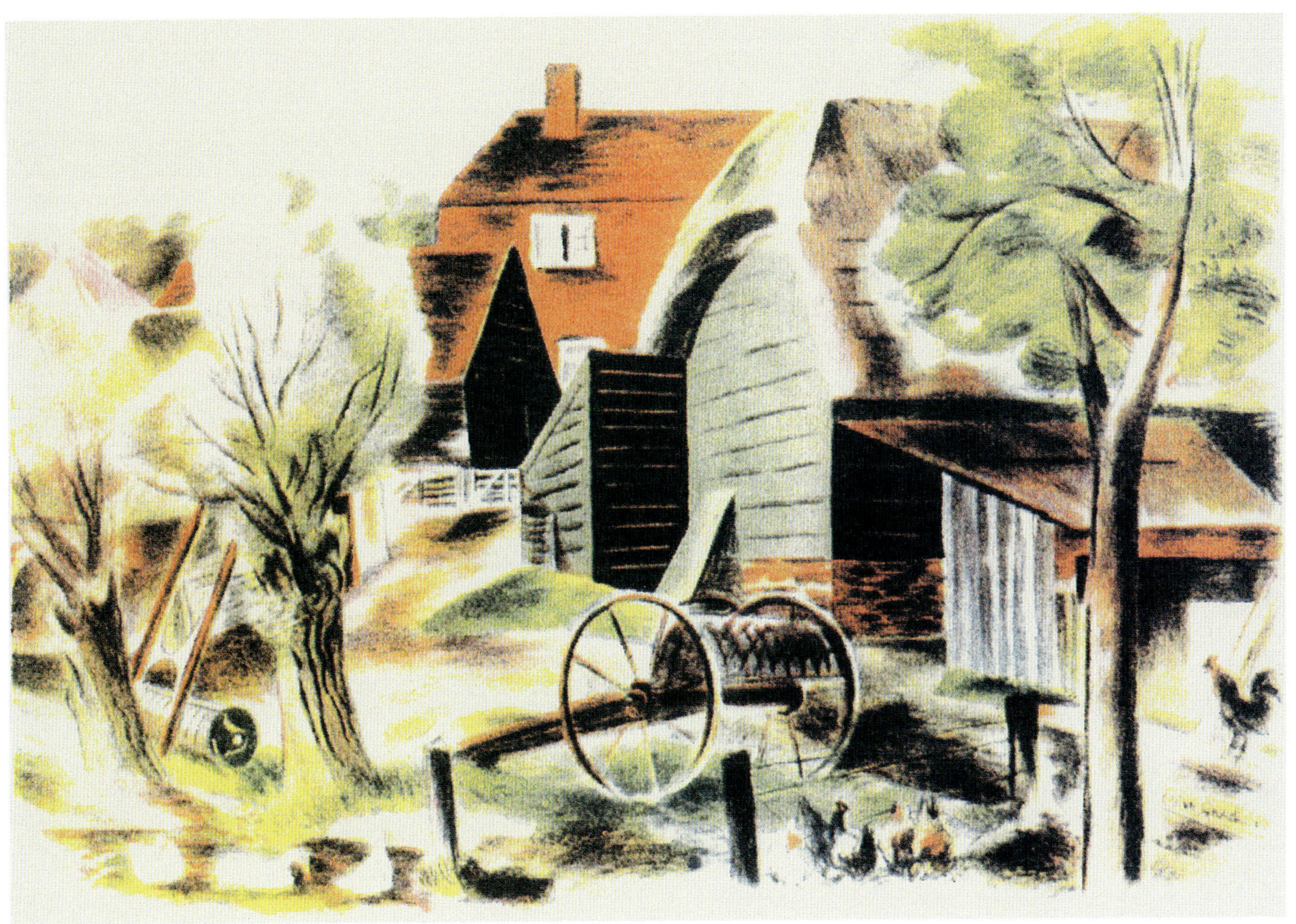

4. *FISHERMAN'S BEACH*, NORAH McGUINESS (1901-1980)

Norah McGuiness was born in Londonderry and studied art in Dublin (1921) before going on to Chelsea (1924) and then to the Academie Lhote in Paris (1929-31).

From 1931 to 1937 she was in London exhibiting with the 7&5 Society and the London Group. In 1937 she went to New York, working on shop window displays. At the onset of war she returned to settle in Dublin. In the 20s she had designed sets and costumes for the Abbey Theatre and for the rest of her life she would supplement her income as an artist by more theatrical work and by providing illustrations for magazines and books (including for Yeats and Elizabeth Bowen).

She became a leading Irish artist of her day, representing Ireland at the Venice Biennale in 1950. Trinity College mounted a retrospective of her work (1968) and gave her an honorary doctorate (1973).

Her first solo exhibition was at the Wertheim Gallery, London (1933); she was to show in London, Dublin and New York.

She painted land- and waterscapes around her favourite area of Dublin Bay. She would swim early and then fill notebooks with charcoal, pencil and watercolour sketches for later working up in the studio.

She had been included in Wellington's mixed shows at Zwemmer's and this, presumably, led to her inclusion in the Contemporary Lithographs project. Her *Fisherman's Beach* would seem typical of her preferred subject matter. She made a clever use of contrasting strong sweeps of colour with white space to silhouette the buildings and to make the centrally shored boat the focus of the print.

Collections

Hugh Lane Gallery of Modern Art, Dublin; Ulster Museum Belfast; Irish Arts Council

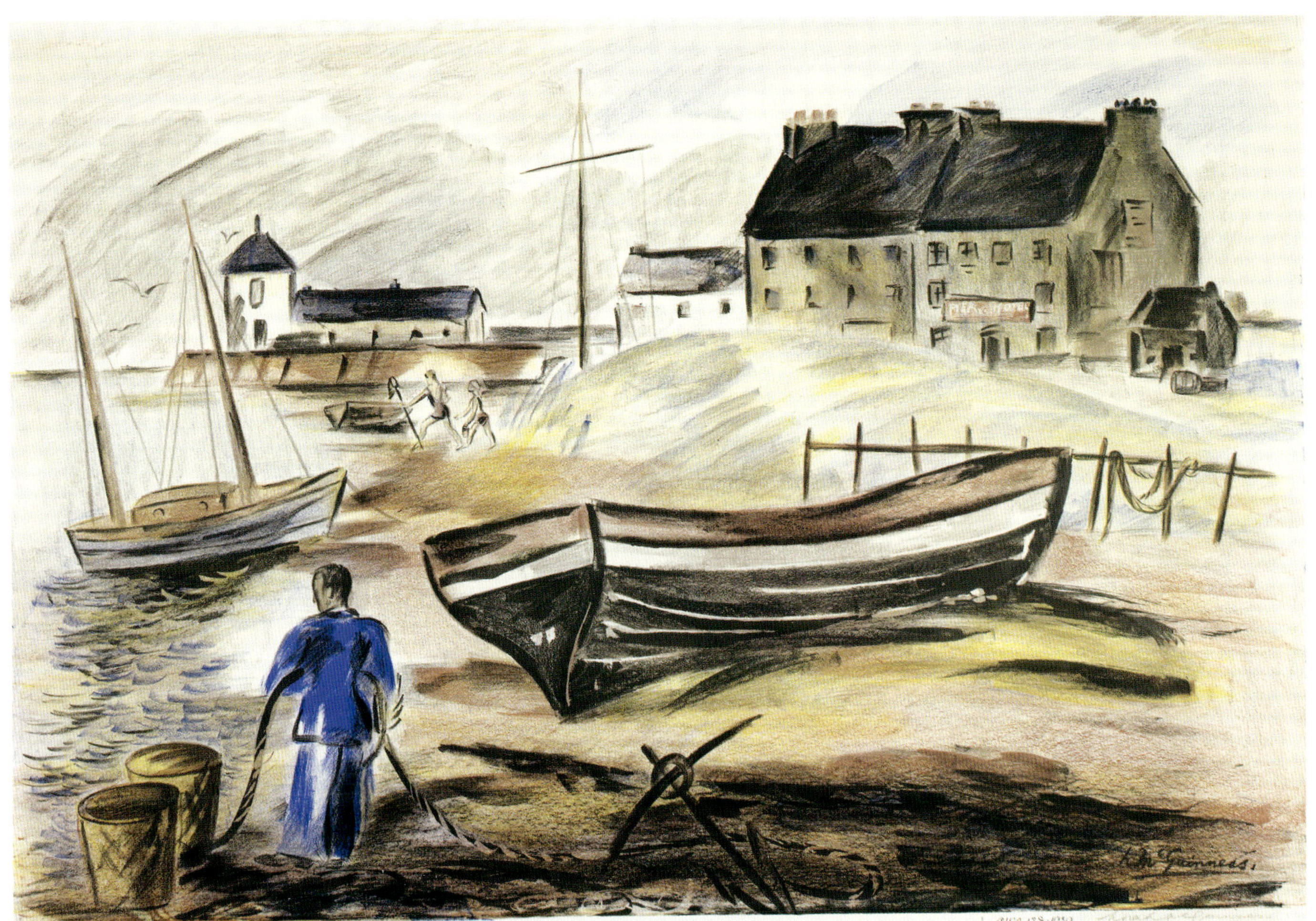

5. *IN THE PARK*, ROBERT MEDLEY (1905-1994)

Robert Medley was born in London and studied at the Byam Shaw School (1923-4), then briefly at the Royal Academy Schools, before settling at the Slade (1924-6) and going on to the Academie Moderne, Paris (1926-8).

On returning to England Medley worked as an assistant to Vanessa Bell and Duncan Grant (1929-34). He was a member of the London Group and of the London Artists' Association. His strong social conscience led him to help establish the Artists International Association and to become designer to the experimental Group Theatre in Cambridge from 1933. Designing for the plays of Auden, Isherwood and Eliot took up much of his non-teaching time in the 30s.

Medley started his distinguished teaching career at Chelsea School of Art in 1932; he worked there through to 1950, apart from his war service in camouflage with the Royal Engineers and later with the British Military Mission in America. He went on to teach painting and stage design at the Slade (1950-58) and became Head of Fine Art at Camberwell (1958-65); in retirement he was appointed Chairman of the Faculty of Painting at the British School in Rome. Of the many students who were influenced by his humanistic teaching were Kitaj, Hockney, Frink and Jarman.

Medley had his first solo show at the Cooling Galleries (1931). He chose to continuously experiment privately rather than to exhibit, but nevertheless he had shows at Lefevre (1948), the Hanover Gallery (1950), and the Leicester Galleries (1960). There was a touring exhibition of his work (1953) and both the Whitechapel (1963) and MOMA, Oxford (1984) gave him retrospectives. Medley received a CBE (1982) and was elected to the RA (1986). John Berger described him as a humanist painter, an unforgettable teacher, and a philosopher.

Medley had links to many of the Contemporary Lithographs Ltd personalities – working for Grant and Bell, teaching at Chelsea alongside Sutherland, associated with Piper and Wellington at the Group Theatre, and showing with Wellington, who owned several of Medley's works. Medley seems to have made a special effort to produce a child accessible lithograph both in subject and style, yet his figures have something of the awkward simplification of his increasingly abstract work of the time.

Collections

The Arts Council, Tate, V&A, National Gallery of Canada, Ottawa

References

1963 Exhibition catalogue, *Robert Medley, retrospective exhibition of paintings, drawings sculpture 1928-63*, Whitechapel Art Gallery

1983 *Robert Medley Drawn from Life*, a memoir, Faber & Faber

2005 *Robert Medley, a centenary tribute*, James Hyman Fine Art Ltd

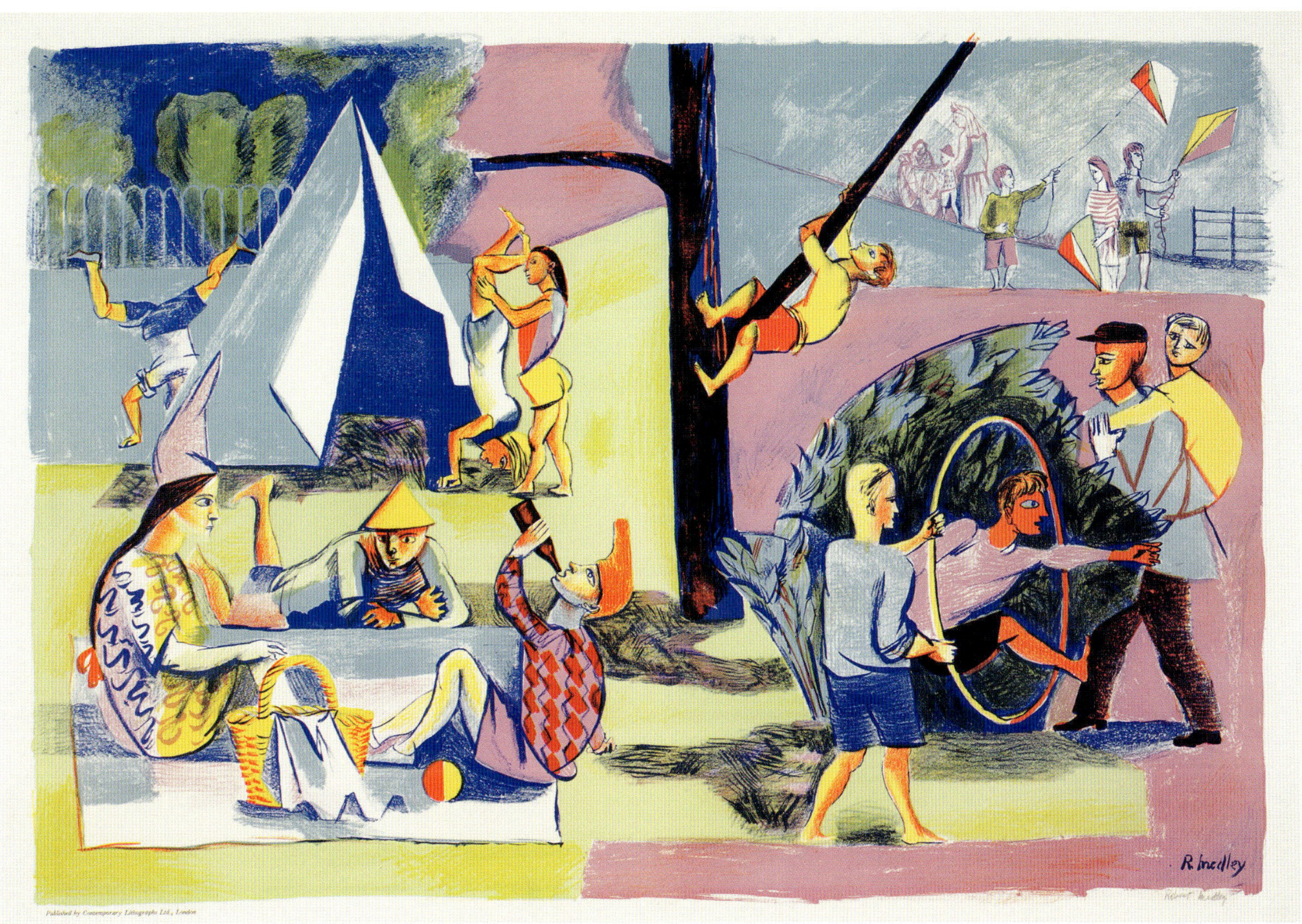
R. Medley
Published by Contemporary Lithographs Ltd., London

6. *THE STOUR AT BURES*, JOHN NASH (1893-1977)

John Nash was born in Kensington, but grew up in Buckinghamshire. Nash had no formal art school training as his brother, Paul, advised against it. He showed with the London Group, the NEAC and with his brother.

In WWI, in 1916, he joined the Artists' Rifles and served on the Western Front until 1918 when he was commissioned as an Official War Artist.

He taught at the Ruskin School of Drawing (1924-29), and then at the RCA (from 1934 – 1958 – apart from WWII period). He became an Honorary Fellow of the RCA.

After retirement he did some teaching at Colchester School of Art.

From 1944 he settled at Wormingford, Essex where he was to live the rest of his life. He devoted himself to gardening and to painting and drawing plants and his surrounding landscape. He described himself as an 'artist-plantsman'.

During WWII he was a war artist to the Admiralty.

Parallel to his plants and landscapes Nash was a prolific illustrator. He contributed to over 60 publications from Lance Sieveking's *Dressing Gowns and Glue* (1919) to *The Natural History of Selborne* (1972). Many of his outstanding pre-WWII illustrations were done in wood engraving. Illustration also gave him scope for his wit and humour.

He became an RA in 1951 and became the first living artist to be given a retrospective there (1967). He received a CBE (1964).

John Nash had done work at the Curwen Press from 1927 when he provided outstanding illustrations for *Poisonous Plants*. Bert Wooton, a Curwen printer, remembered Nash as one of the few artists who would roll up their sleeves and help clean the machines.

Nash's Contemporary Lithograph was of the agricultural landscape running down to the river Stour, near his home. It seems typical of much of his work which he claimed to be representational but 'interested in the structure underneath, though I hope not too obviously'.

Collections

Imperial War Museum

References

1978 John Lewis, *John Nash, the painter as illustrator*, The Pendomer Press

1983 John Rothenstein, *John Nash*, Macdonald & Co.

2006 Brian Webb and Peyton Skipwith, *Design: Paul Nash and John Nash*, Antique Collectors' Club

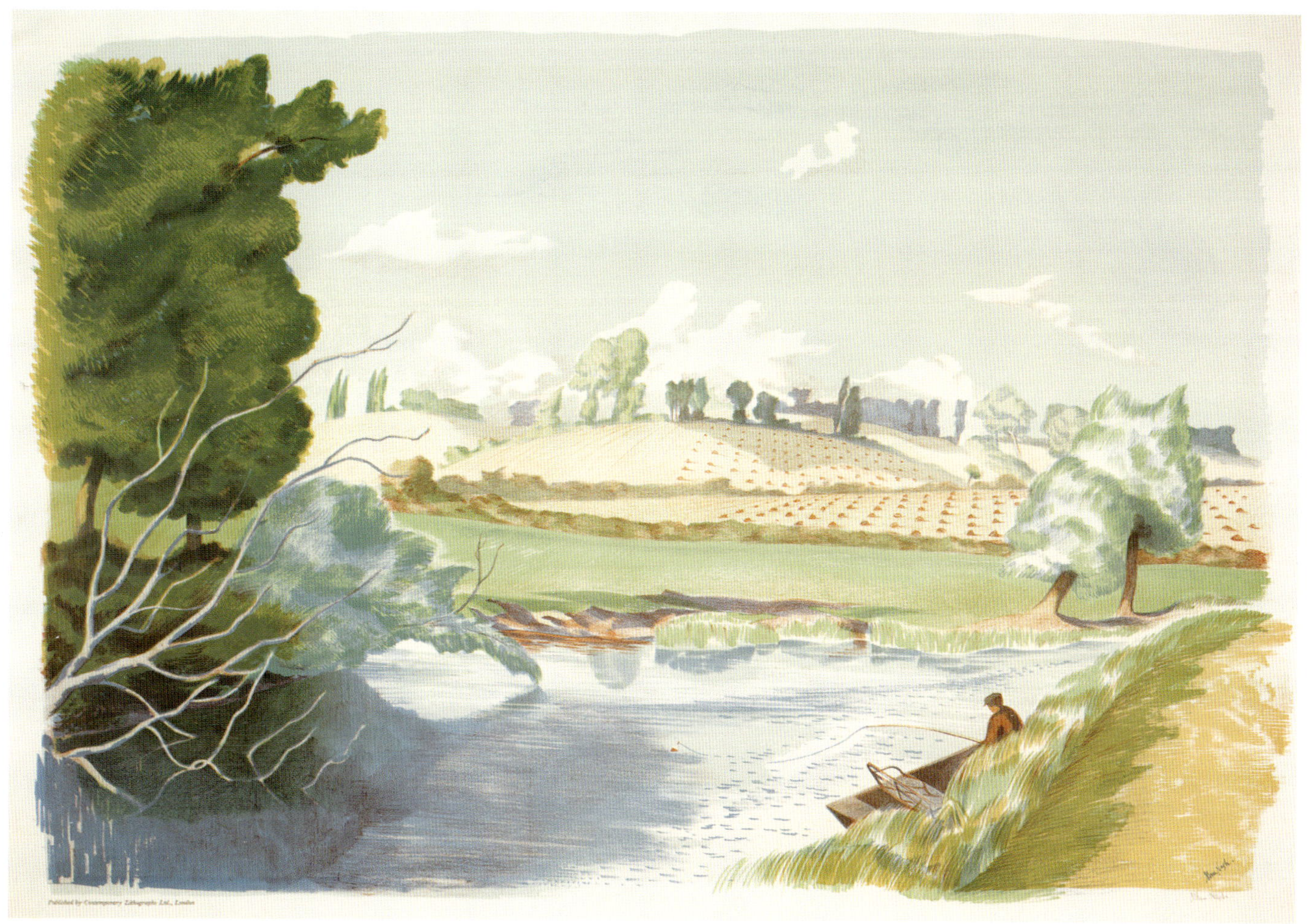

7. *LANDSCAPE OF THE MEGALITHS*, PAUL NASH (1889-1946)

Nash was born in Kensington, London but brought up in Ivor Heath, Buckinghamshire. After short periods at Chelsea and Bolt Court, he studied at the Slade (1910-1911). He had his first solo exhibition, soon after leaving the Slade, at the Carfax Gallery (1912).

In WWI he joined the Artists' Rifles and then was a Lieutenant in the Hampshire Regiment. He was invalided in 1917, and appointed an Official War Artist.

Nash taught for only short periods at the RCA (1924-5 and 1938-40) but nevertheless had a considerable influence on his students, particularly Bawden and Ravilious.

Nash was possibly the most prolific watercolour painter of the inter-war period, although he did work in oils and had a considerable reputation as a wood engraver. Many of his early book illustrations were wood engraving.

Parallel to his art Nash wrote continuously on art and book design, mainly for 'little' magazines. He edited the *Shell Guide* on Dorset for Beddington, and wrote a number of books, four produced posthumously. His *Room and Book* was accompanied by an exhibition at Zwemmer's (1932).

During WWII he, again, was an Official War Artist to the Air Ministry and then to the Ministry of Information.

Ailing since WWI, Nash died prematurely in 1946. The Tate Gallery mounted 'Paul Nash, A Memorial Exhibition' in 1948.

Nash had met Oliver Simon in the 20s and they became lifelong friends and collaborators. Nash contributed to *Signature*, but also contributed to the Pipers' *Axis*. He first worked at the Curwen providing wood engravings for *Genesis* (1924) and for two *Aerial Poems* (1927 & 1929). He also did some borders and publicity for them. Simon found Nash a perfectionist – 'It was always an exciting and unpredictable adventure to work with him and sometimes exhausting for he was wonderfully particular'.

Nash produced four pictures with the title *Landscape of the Megaliths* – an oil, two water colours and his Contemporary Lithograph. He also did many other pictures on associated subjects from his first visit to Avebury in 1933. He reported being totally caught up with the 'dramatic qualities of a composition of shapes equivalent to the prone and upright stones'. His lithograph was to be his last work with the Curwen Press.

Collections

Tate, Imperial War Museum, British Museum, Arts, and British Councils and many provincial Galleries

References

1955 Antony Bertram, *Paul Nash, the portrait of an artist*, Faber & Faber

1973 Margot Eates, *Paul Nash, the master of the image 1889-1946*, John Murray

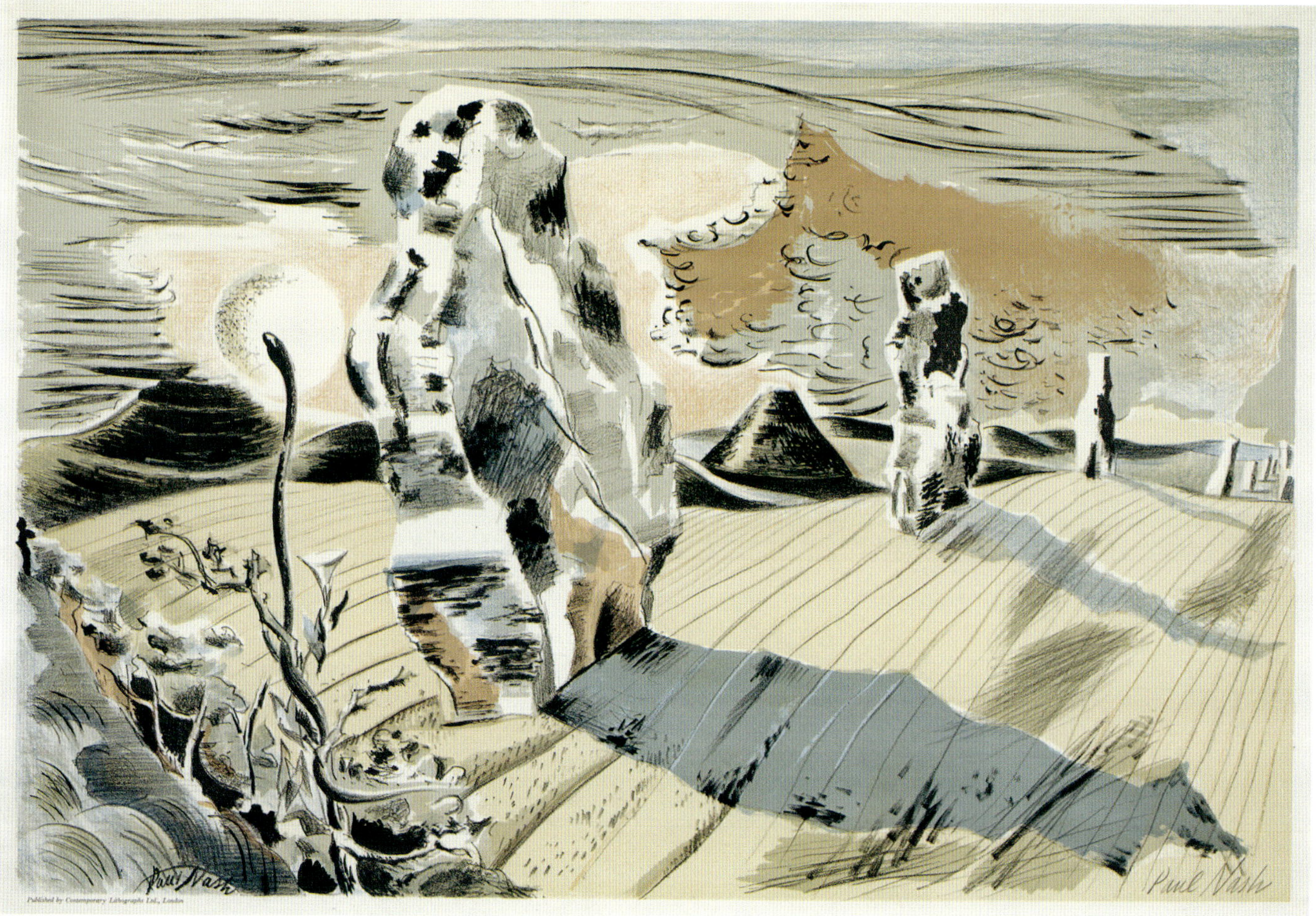
Paul Nash
Published by Contemporary Lithographs Ltd., London
Paul Nash

8. *NEWHAVEN HARBOUR*, ERIC RAVILIOUS (1903-1942)

Eric Ravilious was born in London but grew up in Eastbourne. He was awarded a scholarship to Eastbourne School of Art (1919) and studied at the RCA from 1922 where he won a Design Travelling Scholarship.

From 1921 he developed an interest in wood engraving, influenced by his tutor Paul Nash. He produced wood-engraved illustrations for a number of private presses eg Golden Cockerel and Nonesuch. His most famous book illustrations were for *High Street*, an iconic volume for the period (1937).

Ravilious taught at Eastbourne College of Art from 1925, and, from 1930 at RCA and the Ruskin School of Art. He gave up teaching in 1937.

A mural specialist at RCA, Ravilious was to carry out a number of murals – with Bawden for Morley College (1928-9), and, in the 30s, for the Midland Railway Hotel, Morecambe (1933), and the Colwyn Bay Pier Pavilion (1934). He also took commissions for ceramic decoration, from 1935, designing a number of services – 'Garden', 'Travel', and 'Alphabet' for Wedgwood.

In 1939 he was appointed as Official War Artist with the Admiralty. He worked both in England, and from Norway to the Arctic Circle. His best-known war work was a series of drawings and lithographs of submarines. In 1942 he was reported missing on an air-sea rescue mission.

Ravilious was a considerable water-colourist. He tended to become absorbed in a subject and then paint series. He painted lighthouses along the coast of East Sussex and Kent (his *Newhaven Harbour* contains two). In September 1935 he and Bawden went on a painting excursion to Newhaven, and produced a number of versions of the harbour.

Helen Binyon wrote of Ravilious's Contemporary Lithograph as a 'scene of sensitive clarity and a beautiful luminosity'. Ravilious's title for the lithograph was *Homage to Seurat*. Michael Yorke describes it as 'evoking Seurat's calm and glinting depictions of ports across the Channel'.

Memorial exhibitions were held at The Towner Art Gallery, Eastbourne (1948), The Graves Art Gallery, Sheffield (1958) and at The Minories, Colchester (1972). The Imperial War Museum mounted a major retrospective (2003).

Collections

Imperial War Museum, V&A, the Tate, Towner Art Gallery.

References

1982 Helen Binyon, *Eric Ravilious, memoir of an artist*, Scolar Press

2002 Anne Ullmann (edited), *Ravilious at War*, The Fleece Press

2003 Freda Constable, *The England of Eric Ravilious*, Lund Humphries

2003 Alan Powers, *Eric Ravilious: Imagined Realities*, Imperial War Museum

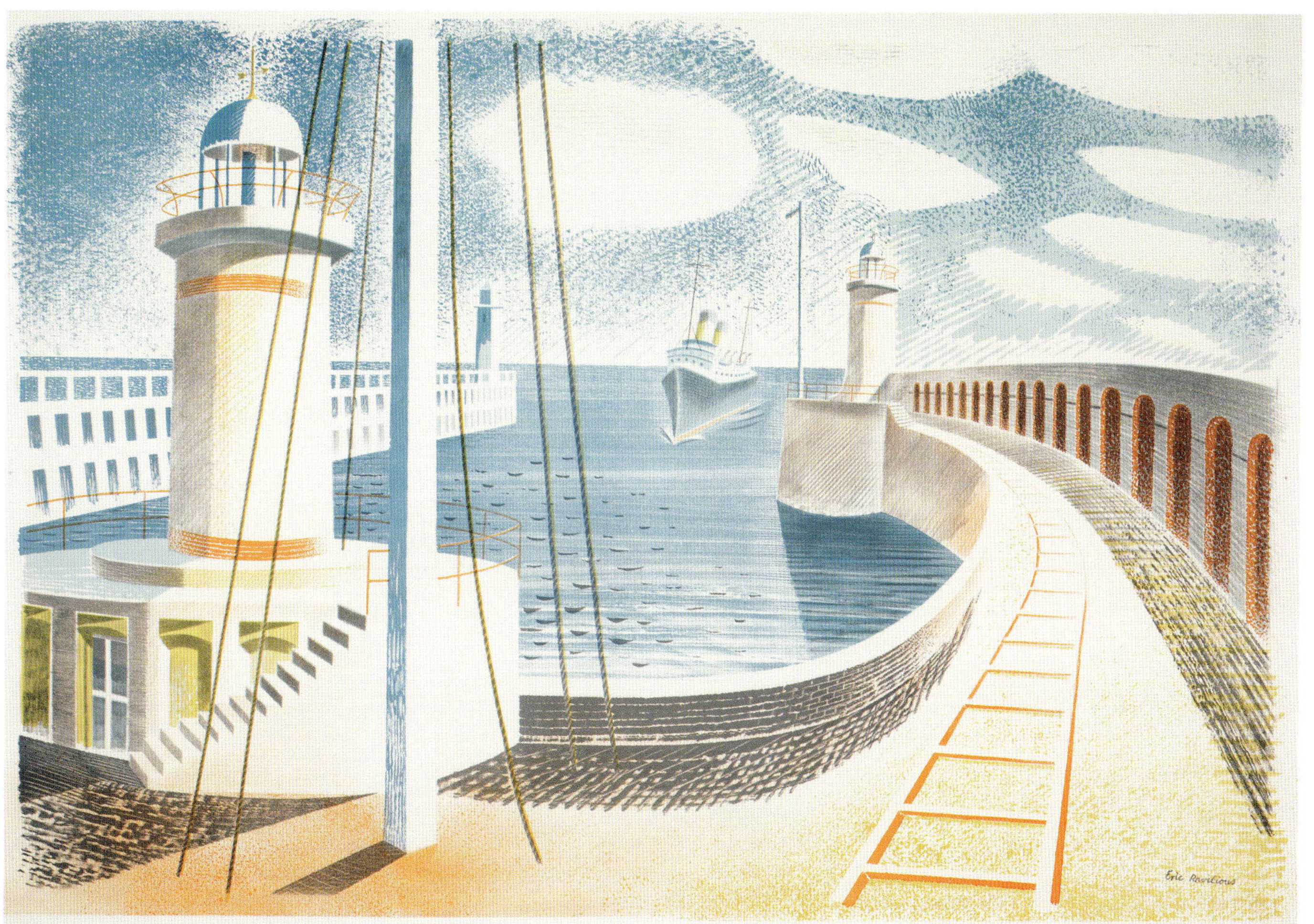
Eric Ravilious

9. *THE SICK DUCK*, GRAHAM SUTHERLAND (1903-1980)

Graham Sutherland was born in Streatham, London but brought up in Sutton, Surrey. In 1937 he settled for the rest of his life in Trottiscliffe, Kent.

He started to train as an engineering apprentice in Derby, but left to study at Goldsmiths (1921-26) where, influenced by the works of Samuel Palmer, he became an etcher. He showed at the Royal Academy whilst still a student.

Sutherland taught, from 1925, at Kingston School of Art and at Chelsea from 1927. At this period, he also took a number of commissions about which he was rather defensive – design work for Milner Gray (tea services and textiles), posters for Shell and London Transport.

Sutherland was not a joiner of artist societies but was lucky enough to have the patronage of Kenneth Clark and Oliver Simon. In the 30s he began to paint in Pembrokeshire and, after the war, in the South of France (where he had a villa from 1955). In WWII he was an Official War Artist commissioned to record the London Blitz and various industrial sites – Cardiff steel works, Derbyshire quarries and Cornish tin mines. He was also to do portraits, triggered by his iconic one of Somerset Maugham (1949). He designed the tapestry for Coventry Cathedral (1962).

Sutherland was one of the few Contemporary Lithographers to achieve international recognition. He showed at the Venice Biennale (1949). He received honorary degrees from Oxford (1962), Leicester (1965) and Cardiff (1979). He was given a retrospective at the Tate (1982).

Sutherland came to Wellington's notice about 1932 and he immediately was asked to show at Zwemmer's and was introduced to Simon, who involved Sutherland in writing for *Signature*. He is recorded to have done a personal Christmas card for Wellington in 1935. Although it is claimed that the *Sick Duck* was his first venture in auto-lithography, it seems he did an auto-lithographed cover for a Curwen Press Newsletter in 1936; whichever, it was to become his preferred method of printing. In 1968 he produced his remarkable bestiary – 26 colour lithographs. As with Williamson's lithograph in the series, Sutherland's anthropomorphic ducks pandered to the young and was a far cry from his original mainstream work which would have been more likely to stimulate children's imaginations.

Collections

Tate and major out-of-London galleries

References

1980 John Hayes, *The Art of Graham Sutherland*, Phaidon

1982 Roger Berthoud, *Graham Sutherland: a biography*, Faber & Faber

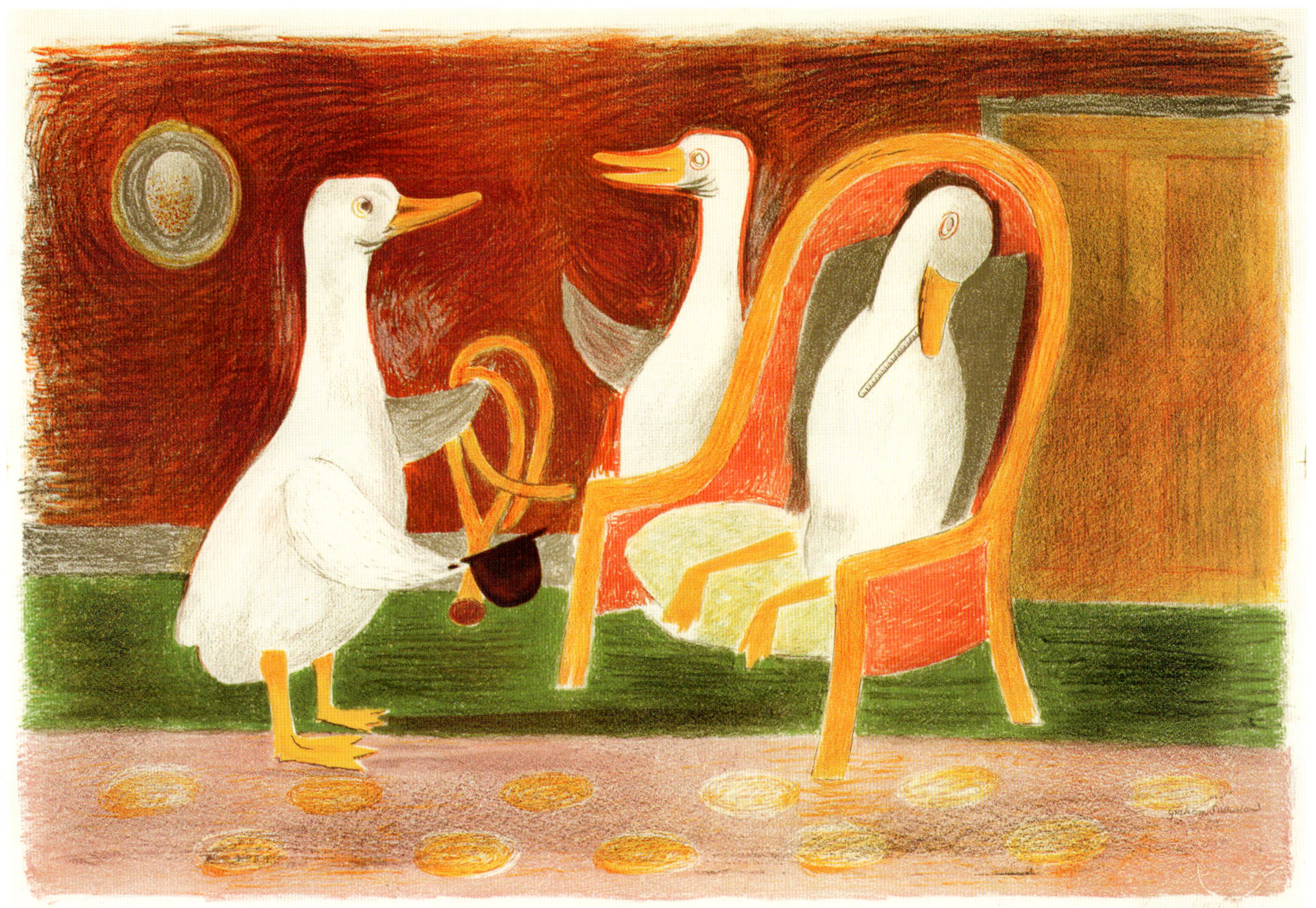

10. *BEARS AT TEA*, HAROLD WILLIAMSON (1892-1978)

Harold Williamson was born in Leeds, attending Leeds School of Art (1911-1914); he went on to the Royal Academy Schools (1914-15) where he won the Turner Gold Medal.

It is not clear whether Williamson actually did work for the War Artists Scheme in WWI, as he was appointed at the end of the war. For most of the war he served as a rifleman on the Western Front and was badly wounded. He is said to have kept illustrated diaries in the trenches, whilst reading Ruskin! What work he did produce during the war focused on the role animals played.

During the 30s Williamson became a well-known poster artist providing work for London Transport and the Post Office, where he was the first to be commissioned for a series of posters specifically for schools.

He became Head of Chelsea School of Art in 1932 and was to remain there until his retirement in 1958. He was an energetic and adventurous principal, setting up a sculpture school employing Henry Moore, and employing young artists as teachers, Sutherland, Claude Rogers and Ceri Richards (of whom he became a collector).

Williamson's second love was music and he wrote and illustrated a paperback – *The Orchestra*.

That Williamson had his potential audience very much in mind when given a commission was exemplified with his Post Office school posters – 'the appeal being to a multitude of boys who would be certain to possess mechanical rather than aesthetic interest. I thought it desirable that there should be the maximum factual content, and the artistic treatment must be a secondary consideration'. The results were exactly that – historically and technically interesting pictures with little aesthetic merit.

With his Contemporary Lithograph *Bears at Tea* unfortunately Williamson seems again to have put centrally what he thought young children may have liked, producing what nowadays appears to be a particularly mawkish, anthropomorphic image which could have had little impact of pupils' appreciation of 'good' art.

Collections

Imperial War Museum, Post Office Archives

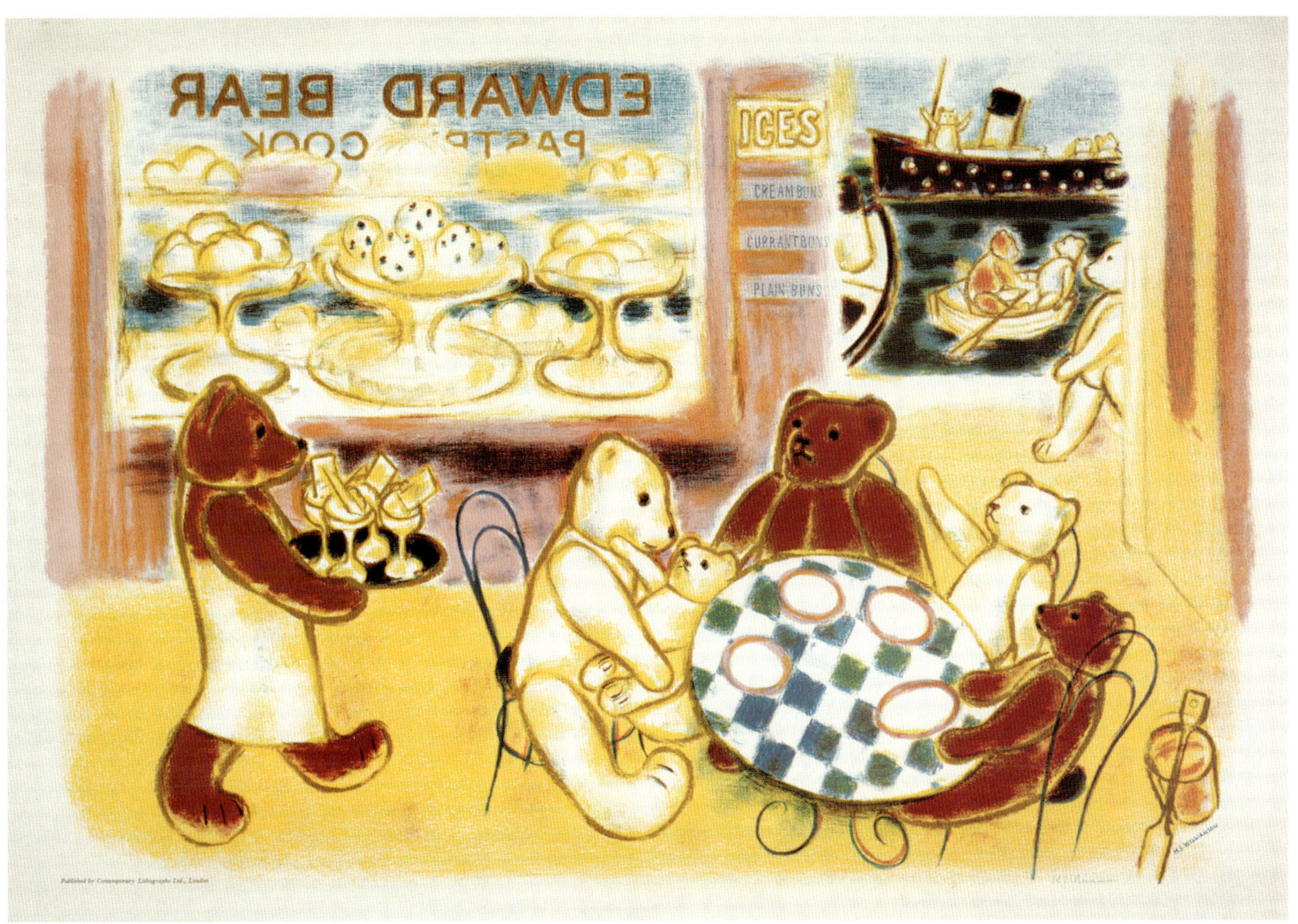
EDWARD BEAR
ICES
CREAM BUNS
CURRANT BUNS
PLAIN BUNS
H.S. WILLIAMSON
Published by Contemporary Lithographs Ltd., London

CONTEMPORARY LITHOGRAPHS

Series Two (March 1938)

11. *Mill in Essex* John Aldridge
12. *The Bus Stop* Edward Ardizzone
13. *The Schoolroom* Vanessa Bell
14. *Landscape in the Lake District* Raymond Coxon
15. *At the Ballet* Duncan Grant
16. *Still Life* Ivon Hitchens
17. *Arrangement of Jugs* Frances Hodgkins
18. *Grand Junction Canal* Lynton Lamb
19. *Skating* Vincent Lines
20. *Abstract Composition* John Piper
21. *The Thames at Chiswick* Mary Potter
22. *Greenwich Hospital* Randolph Schwabe
23. *Imaginary Harbour* Edward Wadsworth
24. *Nursery frieze – Seascape* John Piper
25. *Nursery frieze – Landscape* John Piper

SERIES TWO

11. *MILL IN ESSEX*, JOHN ALDRIDGE (1905-1983)

Aldridge had no formal art training but was a classical scholar at Corpus Christi College, Oxford (1925-28). He started painting whilst at Oxford and a private income enabled him to become a full-time artist on leaving college. He travelled widely in Europe but in 1933 settled, for the rest of his life, in Great Bardfield, Essex, in a grand Elizabethan house. He soon became associated with local artists and was to collaborate with Edward Bawden in designing wallpaper for Coles.

During WWII he worked as a photographic interpreter in the Intelligence Corps.

In 1949 William Coldstream invited him to teach part-time at the Slade (1949-1970). In 1963 he was elected to the Royal Academy.

Although he did some portraiture, Aldridge largely painted his local villages and landscapes. Betjeman wrote of him – 'He belongs to an English tradition of local pastoral artists... He is also the gardeners' artist. You can see that he is happy in every part of his garden at Great Bardfield, looking at the vegetables as well as the flowers; the winter as well as the summer...'

Aldridge's Contemporary Lithograph seems typical of his work, making no particular concessions to the targeted educational market.

Collections

Tate, V&A, Fry Art Gallery, Saffron Walden

References

2003 Martin Salisbury (ed.), *Artists at the Fry*, The Ruskin Press/ Fry Art Gallery

2005 Malcolm Yorke, *The Inward Laugh, Edward Bawden and his circle*, The Fleece Press

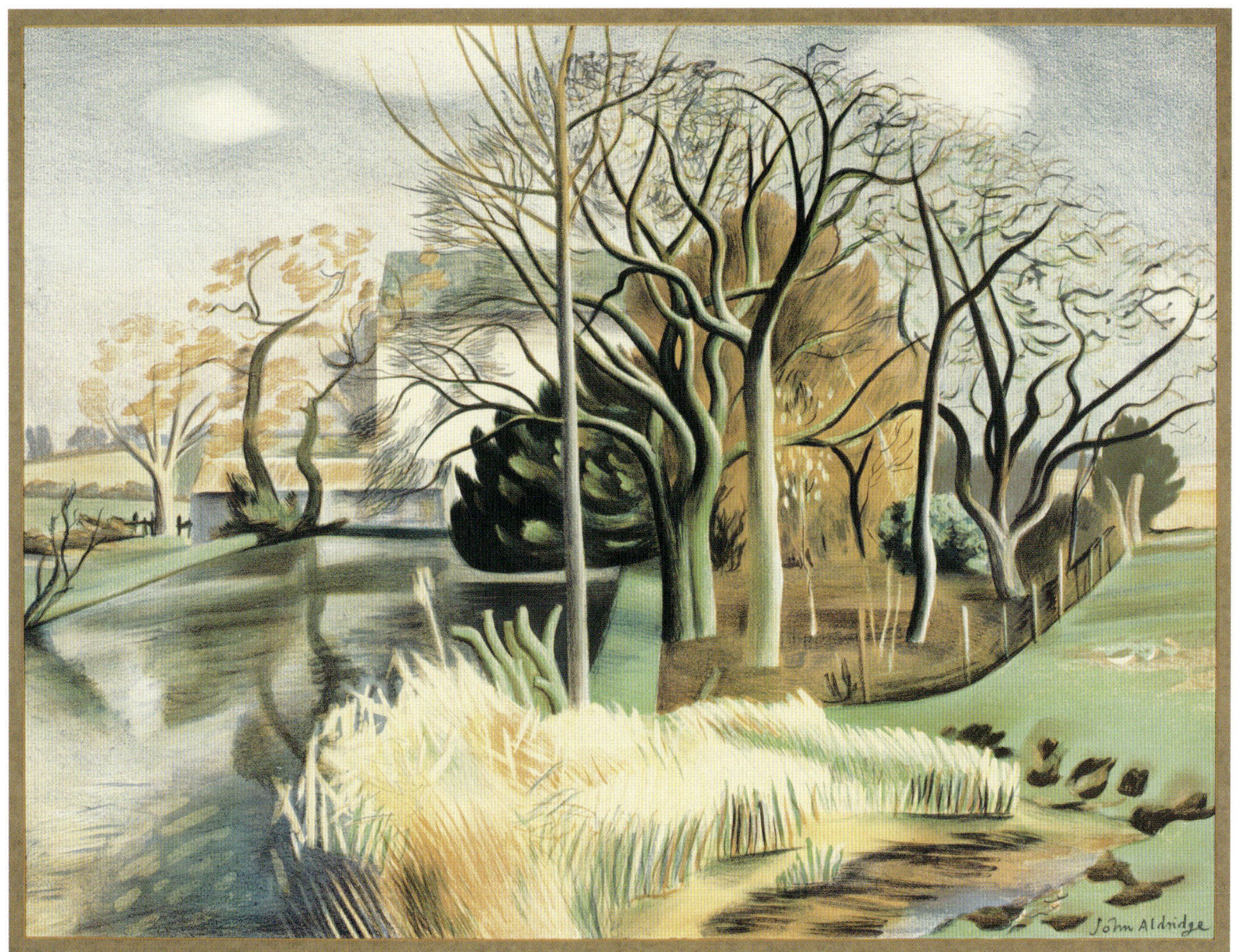
John Aldridge

12. *THE BUS STOP*, EDWARD ARDIZZONE (1900-1978)

Edward Ardizzone was born in French Indo-China but was brought up in London where he was to spend most of his life. He did not attend art school on a full time basis but took evening classes at Westminster School of Art for many years whilst working as a clerk (1919-26). In 1927 he decided to become a full time artist.

Edward Ardizzone was a major book illustrator, both of his own books and of others. *In a Glass Darkly* was the first book he illustrated (1929). His own first book *Little Tim and the Brave Sea Captain* was written and illustrated in 1936. In all, he illustrated some 180 books. In 1956 he won the Kate Greenaway and Hans Christian Anderson Medal for his work with children's books.

During WWII he was a major Official War Artist producing some 400 works and recording his memoirs. He taught at Camberwell (1948-53) and at the RCA from 1953. He was elected to the Royal Academy (1948-53); was made a CBE (1971); and was elected Royal Designer for Industry (1974).

His lithography tended to be in monochrome. Paul Caldwell wrote of his work – 'Ardizzone's lithographs are beautiful examples of the quality of chalk drawing. There is a sense...of the delight in the touch of the crayon on to the surface, whether it be stone or plate'.

Much of his working life was recording the daily round of folk in the surroundings of Maida Vale. *The Bus Stop* is typical of his reportage. The altercation of the bus conductor with the plump woman (his women tended to be Rubenesque) is typical of the sharp humour of his social commentary.

Bibliography

1974 Exhibition catalogue, *Edward Ardizzone, a retrospective exhibition*, V&A

1979 Gabriel White, *Edward Ardizzone: artist and illustrator*, The Bodley Head

2000 Nicholas Ardizzone, *Edward Ardizzone's World*, Unicorn Press

2003 Brian Alderson, *Edward Ardizzone, a bibliographic commentary*, Oak Knoll Press/Private Libraries Association

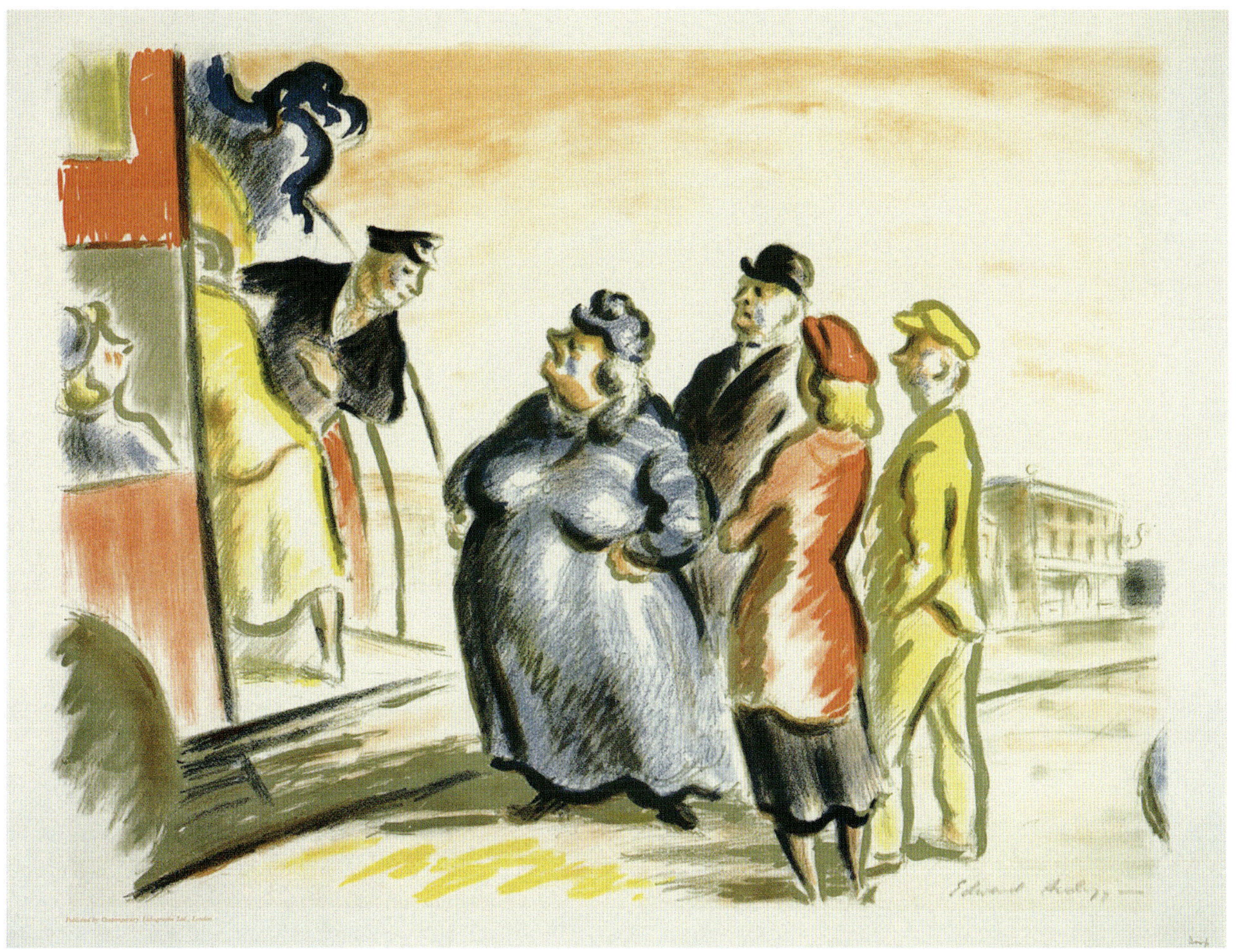

13. *THE SCHOOLROOM*, VANESSA BELL (1879-1961)

Vanessa Bell was a well-established painter and designer by the time she was commissioned by Wellington and Piper. She was a central personality in the Bloomsbury Circle of painters and writers, and was closely associated, for much of her life, with Duncan Grant, with whom she shared a home, a child, and many decorative commissions. The two were to 'hold court' variously at Gordon Square, Charleston and Cassis, France.

Bell attended the Royal Academy Schools from 1901. She married the art critic Clive Bell and was soon caught up with his 'significant form' and with Roger Fry's popularisation of Post-Impressionist art. Bell also produced textiles, screens etc for Fry's Omega Workshop.

Although perhaps characterised as a 'fine' artist of domestic scenes, with interest in pattern and colour, Bell frequently took commissions for 'commercial' designs. She produced dinner service designs for Foleys and for Wilkinson & Co; she did the odd poster for the likes of Shell and the Post Office, some theatrical work, and dust jackets for the Hogarth Press (including many for the books of her sister, Virginia Woolf). The Arts Council mounted a touring exhibition of her work in 1964.

No reference is made to Bell's Contemporary Lithograph in Spalding's biography. It was Bell's wont to include her friends and relatives in her work as, for example, in her *Nursery Interior with Two Women* and *Nursery Tea*. In *Schoolroom* one might possibly see portraits of herself, her sister writing, and her daughter, Angelica, at her devoirs. The lithograph is a good example of Bell's interest in patterns and textures (stemming from her Omega work) and her liking for strong colours – blues, purples and vermilions, that she was to prefer for her own clothes as well as on her canvases.

References

1983 Frances Spalding, *Vanessa Bell*, Weidenfeld & Nicolson

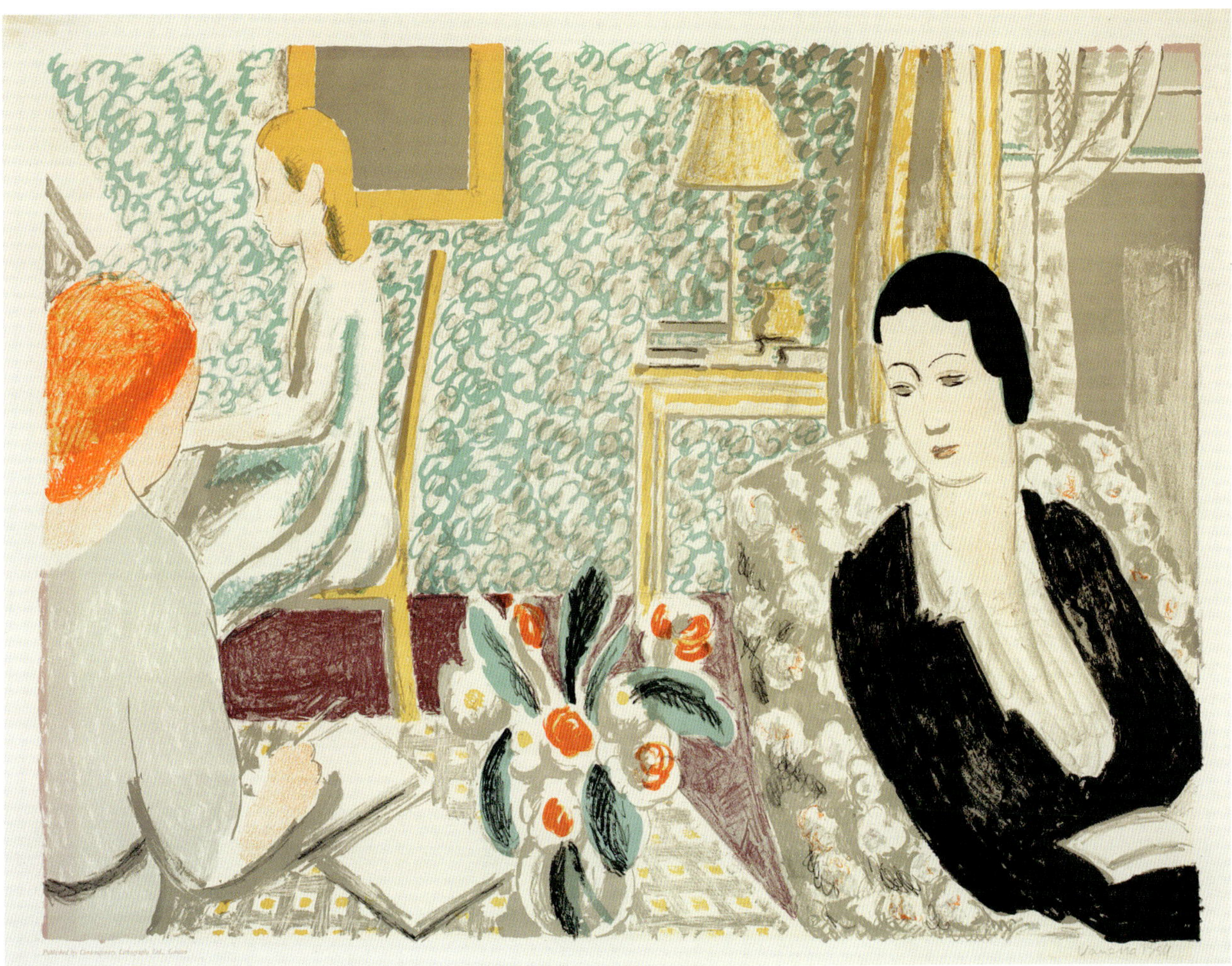

14. *LANDSCAPE IN THE LAKE DISTRICT.* RAYMOND COXON (1896-1997)

Raymond Coxon was born in Hanley, near Stoke-on-Trent. Immediately on leaving school he served with the Cavalry in Palestine during WWI (1915-18). He first studied at Leeds College of Art (1919-21), (where he was a fellow student of Henry Moore) before going on to the RCA. (1921-25), along with Bawden, Ravilious and Freedman. Whilst there, he painted a mural for the Royal College 'The Expulsion from Eden' . He went with Moore to France where he studied at Colorosi's atelier, and was to share a studio with Moore on leaving college. He and Moore helped found the British Independent Society (1927), an exhibiting society.

Coxon taught part-time at Richmond College of Art, where Piper was his pupil.(Piper was later to write the foreword in the catalogue for Coxon's retrospective exhibition). He also taught variously at Chelsea, Guilford, Kingston and Hammersmith schools of art, retiring from teaching in 1971. Piper was to describe him as dedicated, sensitive, open-minded and easy going but a shade too tempted by 'isms'. In 1932 he wrote *Art, An Introduction to Appreciation*, part of Pitmans' *Art and Life* series.

During WWII he was an Official War Artist.

As a painter Coxon tended to have landscapes as his subject matter. He was interested in the mythical, folklorish interpretations of the countryside. Coxon also did some portraiture, but mainly of friends and family. He had been influenced by Cézanne and this is clear in his lithograph both in style and colour. The strong colours would have seemed attractive to children and their eyes would have been drawn to the ploughman and his very white horse.

Coxon contributed to other series of lithographs eg those of AIA and made a lithograph for NAAFI that was distributed to its canteens worldwide.

Collections

Tate, Manchester, British Museum, V&A

References

1985 Exhibition catalogue, *Raymond Coxon and Edna Ginesi*, Parkin Gallery

1987 Exhibition catalogue, *Raymond Coxon, retrospective*, Stoke-on-Trent City Museum and Art Gallery

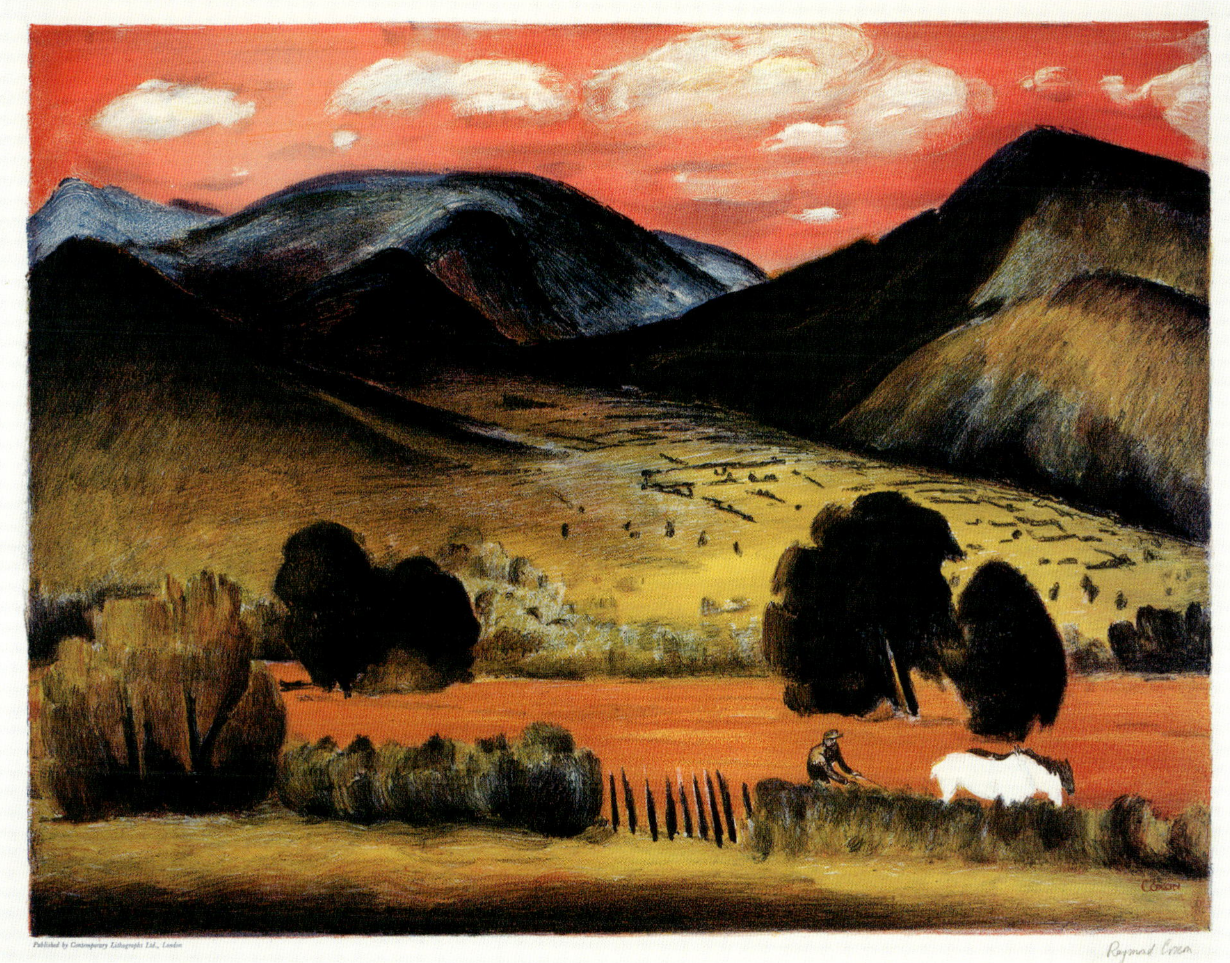
COXON
Published by Contemporary Lithographs Ltd., London
Raymond Coxon

15. *AT THE BALLET*, DUNCAN GRANT (1885-1978)

Duncan Grant had a rather haphazard art education, attending, for short periods, Westminster School of Art and the Slade.

Being partly brought up with his cousins, the Stracheys, he was drawn into the Bloomsbury Group, showing in Fry's Post-Impressionist Exhibition (1912) and taking part in his Omega workshop. Grant's mural for Borough Polytechnic brought him a wider audience.

Grant was to live with Vanessa Bell, at Charleston and later their cottage at Cassis as his base, travelling widely. He undertook many and varied 'decorative' commissions – murals, textiles, furniture, books – alongside his main preoccupation with painting.

He had an early interest in ballet, from when he lived in Paris. His friendship with Maynard Keynes led to work with the Diaghelev Ballet. He was to paint Keyne's wife, the ballet dancer, Lydia Lopokova, and to have dancing as a theme for some of his paintings.

Frances Spalding wrote of Grant's Contemporary Lithograph – '...plays on the contrast, in colour and movement, between audience and stage, with brilliantly lit ballet dancers flitting like birds above the serried rows of seated figures. As with the other prints in the series, the choice of subject pandered to the English love of the familiar and anecdotal'. Grant was later to do two more lithographs at the Curwen for the Observer Prints, where he was helped by the printer Stanley Jones to do the colour separations, suggesting that he may have needed similar help from Piper when doing his Contemporary Lithograph.

Grant was given a retrospective exhibition at the Tate (1959) and at the Scottish National Gallery of Modern Art (1975).

References

1948 Raymond Mortimer, *Duncan Grant*, Penguin Modern Painters

1997 Frances Spalding, *Duncan Grant*, Chatto & Windus

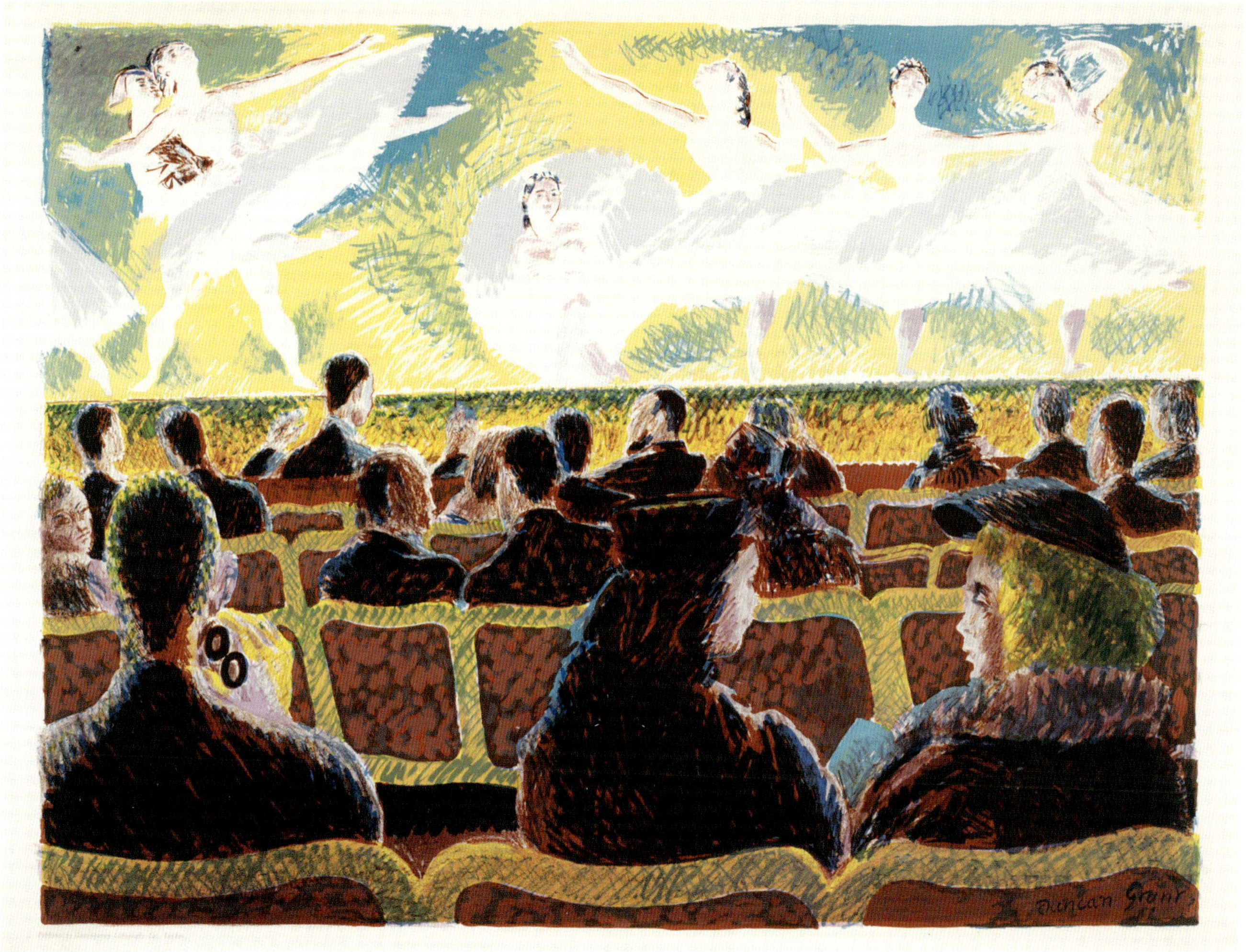

16. *STILL LIFE*, IVON HITCHENS (1893-1979)

Ivon Hitchens was born in London. After a year at St John's Wood Art School he had three periods at the Royal Academy Schools (1911-12,1914-16, and 1918-1919).

The inter-war years saw Hitchens active in various of the art societies of the time – he took part in all the exhibitions of the 7&5 Society and was a member of the London Artist's Association, the London Group and the Society of Mural Painters (he was to do several church murals).

He had his first solo exhibition at the Mayor Gallery (1925) and had more than ten solo shows at the Leicester Galleries from 1940. In 1956 he represented Britain at the Venice Biennale. He received a CBE (1958) . He was given a major Arts Council retrospective at the Tate (1964) and another at the Royal Academy (1979).

In 1939, to escape the Blitz, Hitchens bought land in Sussex, and for the rest of his life painted from his immediate surroundings. Influenced by the Post-Impressionists, from 1924 he chose to paint in strong coloured oils. He aimed to reduce his subject matter to 'patches and lines of pigment', seeking essences on long horizontal canvases. From the 40s he approached nude painting in a similar manner. He is generally branded as a neo-romantic.

Hitchens's *Still Life* was his only venture into lithography. Peter Khoroche describes it as 'a relaxed, airy piece, loosely drawn...on a cream background, with white areas for the eye to rest in between the superimposed areas of yellow, blue, mauve, green and rust.' The lithograph does not seem particularly typical of the rest of Hitchens's work lacking his usual broad strong colour strokes and containing thin lines for the stems and heads of his flowers.

Collections

Tate and major UK galleries

References

1990 Peter Khoroche, *Ivon Hitchens*, Andre Deutsch

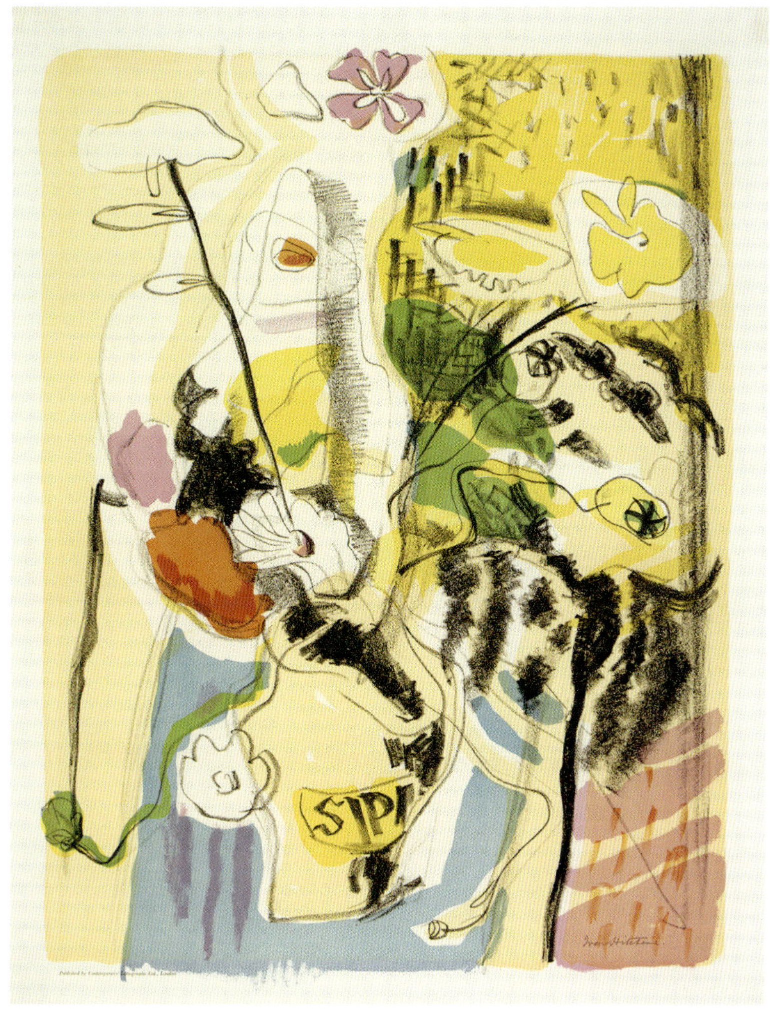

17. *ARRANGEMENT OF JUGS*, FRANCES HODGKINS (1869-1947)

Frances Hodgkins was born in Dunedin, New Zealand and attended the school of art there from 1895. She worked there, for a time, illustrating magazines and newspapers.

From 1901 she came to Europe and from then on moved between England, the Continent and New Zealand restlessly, showing in mixed and solo exhibitions interspersed in the early days with some teaching. She had settled periods variously in different parts of London, Cornwall and Dorset.

Apart from a short period working as a textile designer for the Calico Printing Association in Manchester (1925-6) Hodgkins earned her living as a painter. In 1929 she was elected to the 7&5 Society and had a short spell with Unit One. In all she was to have more than 30 solo exhibitions at the St George's Gallery, the Leicester Galleries and at Lefevre. In 1940 she showed 40 works at the Venice Biennale. The Arts Council held a memorial exhibition of her work (1952). She developed from a minor provincial painter in New Zealand to a leading British one, continuously experimenting, not finding her personal style until her 60s. She described it as 'liberating still life from its domestic setting'.

Wellington had included Hodgkins in his mixed shows at Zwemmer's and Paul Nash used her work in his exhibition there – *Room and Book*. The Pipers were to become close friends, looking after her when she was ill in 1942, negotiating a Civil List pension for her, and Myfanwy Piper wrote a short monograph on Hodgkins for Penguin.

Griffits described Hodgkins's Contemporary Lithograph as characterised by 'crisp floating shapes held in tension with patches and sweeps of clear colour: a brilliant cadmium yellow singing out next to a primary red contributes to a particularly light, buoyant image. Its colouring and emphasis on sharpish vertical shapes has something in common with John Piper's contribution to the series...' Piper thought Hogkins's lithograph made the others look 'tame and school-girlish' (but then he had worked with her on it!). It is her only surviving print.

Collections

Tate Gallery, Dunedin Public Art Gallery, Auckland City Art Gallery.

References

1995 Ian Buchanan, Michael Dunn, Elizabeth Eastmond, *Frances Hodgkins, paintings and drawings*, Thames and Hudson

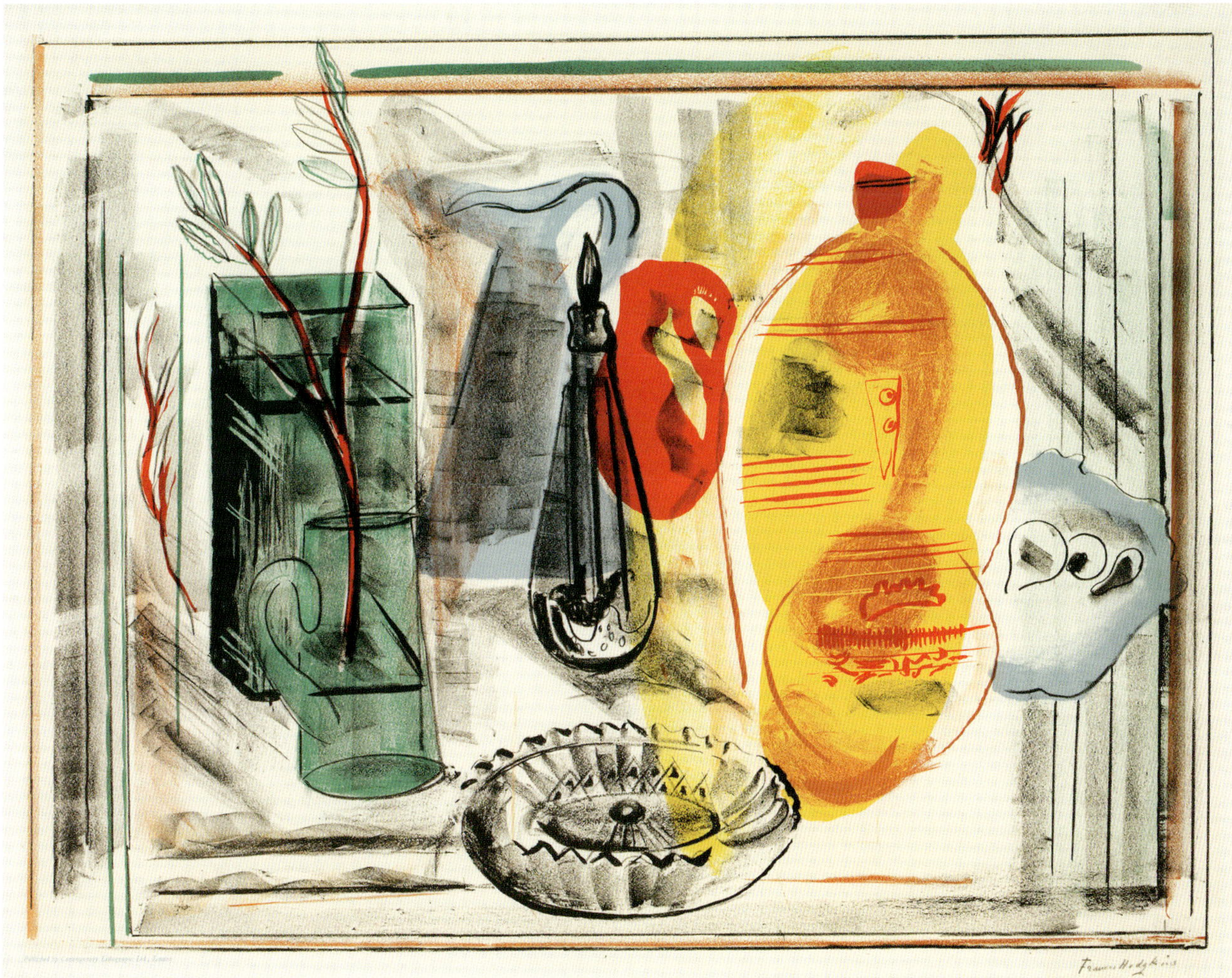

18. *GRAND JUNCTION CANAL*, LYNTON LAMB (1907-1977)

Lynton lamb was born in Hyderabad, India, but brought up in Blackheath. Whilst working as an estate agent he attended, part-time, Randolph Schwabe's classes at Camberwell. He went on to study at Central School of Arts and Crafts (1928-30) – engraving with Noel Rooke and lithography with A.S.Hartrick. With Lethaby's philosophy of generalisation Lamb tested himself out with different media. Later he took classes in book-binding under Douglas Cockerell and was to succeed him as tutor in the School of Book Production (1935-39). After WWII Lamb became Head of Lithography at the Slade (1950-71) and worked part-time at RCA (1956-70).

On leaving Central, Lamb joined Oxford University Press, designing prayer books and bibles and book jackets. In WWII he was commissioned in the Royal Engineers, working in camouflage. He had done his first book illustration in 1929 and, returning to OUP after the war, he was appointed art editor for their illustrated Trollopes. When he left OUP he acted as their typography consultant. In all Lamb was to illustrate some 60 books, 20 published by OUP.

Lamb became a Fellow of the Royal Society of Arts (1953), a Fellow of the Society of Industrial Artists (1968) and a Royal Designer for Industry (1974).

Lamb called Hartrick's teaching of lithography as 'a benison laying on of hands'; Lamb particularly like the direct contact of auto-lithography. He tended to do meticulous studies and tracing beforehand so that his confidence when coming to the stone led to few alterations. This confidence, along with his interest in commonplace scenes shows well in his *Grand Junction Canal* with the man, woman and child, each charmingly preoccupied with their own chores.

Lamb's work at the Curwen Press led to his post-war contributions to *Signature*, and to lithographs for books printed there. He was to write – 'When I was a young man to those of us who used to work on the stone with Wally Gapp at North St, Plaistow...the good opinion of Harold Curwen and Oliver Simon was very valuable...'

References

1947 John Lewis, *The Drawings and Book Decorations of Lynton Lamb*, Alphabet & Image

1979 G.Mackie, *Lynton Lamb: illustrator*, Scolar Press

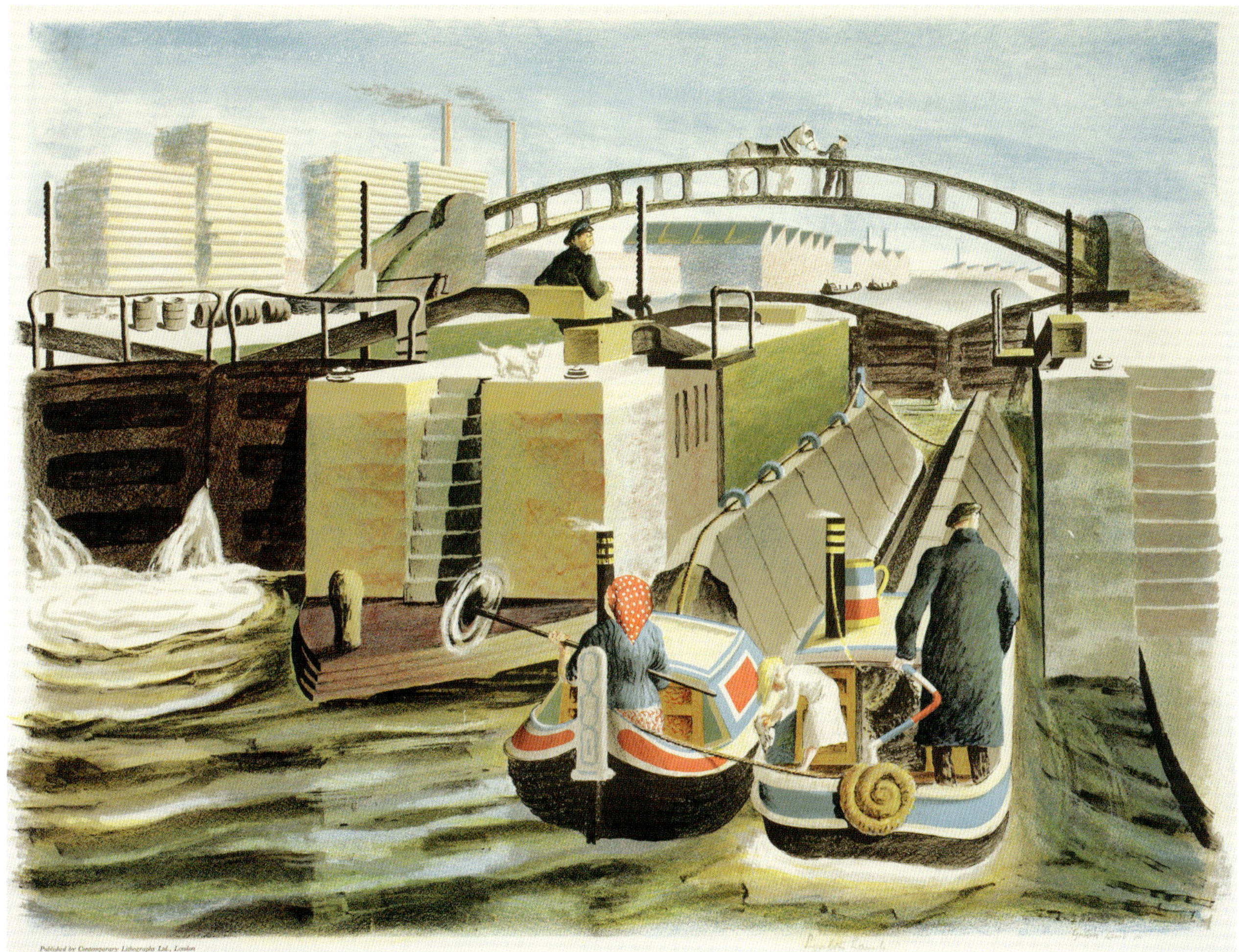
Published by Contemporary Lithographs Ltd., London

19. *SKATING*, VINCENT LINES (1910-1968)

Vincent Lines was born in Dulwich. He studied etching, engraving and lithography at the Central School of Arts and Crafts under A.S.Hartrick. Lines gained a scholarship to RCA (1928) and won a travelling scholarship there in 1932. William Rothenstein rated Lines one of the best students of his year.

Lines was a great walker and cyclist with the instincts of a countryman; he toured and recorded scenes all round Great Britain and in France. He eventually had a Mobylette, which he kept in his farmhouse in Vauclose.

After teaching in Manchester and Bradford, he became Principal of Horsham School of Art (1935-44). He then moved to become Principal of Hastings Municipal School of Arts and Crafts in 1945, where he worked until his premature death. The Vincent Lines Memorial Trust gives an annual prize in his memory.

Lines was a major water-colourist, contributing to the *Recording Britain* project. He did some book illustration and wrote *Shaping and Making* for schools, on country crafts. He was described as a 'gentle' painter of local scenes, and said of himself that he 'wished to purvey the tranquillity of God'.

Lines had worked with lithography from his student days; he is even said to have carried a stone with him on his travels sometimes. He did a lithograph of his teacher, Hartrick, in 1932. Lines had painted winter scenes around his home in Sussex from the 20s; presumably *Skating* was a familiar image for him. Although it has been criticised as being no more than an insipid sketch, it has a real humour (somewhat lacking in others of the series) and figures of mother and children to which pupils could easily relate.

Collections

V&A, Royal Collection, British Council, National Galleries of Ireland and Wales,

References

1975 Exhibition Catalogue, *Vincent Lines Memorial Exhibition*, Hastings Museum and Art Gallery

1980 Exhibition Catalogue, *Drawn from Nature*, South East Arts

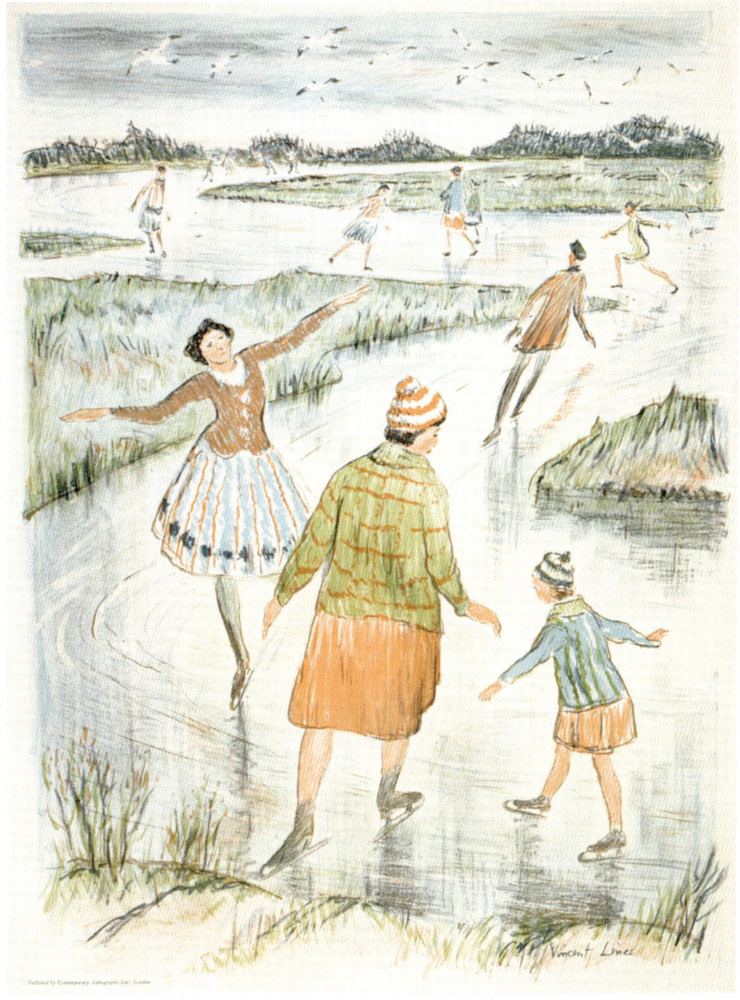
Vincent Lines

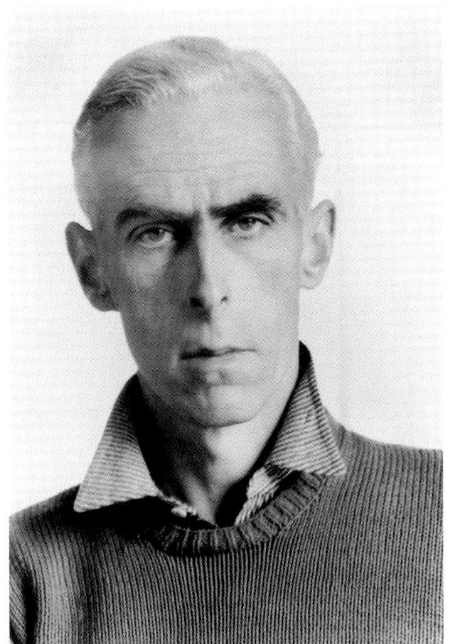

John Piper

20. *Abstract Composition*, John Piper (1903-1992)

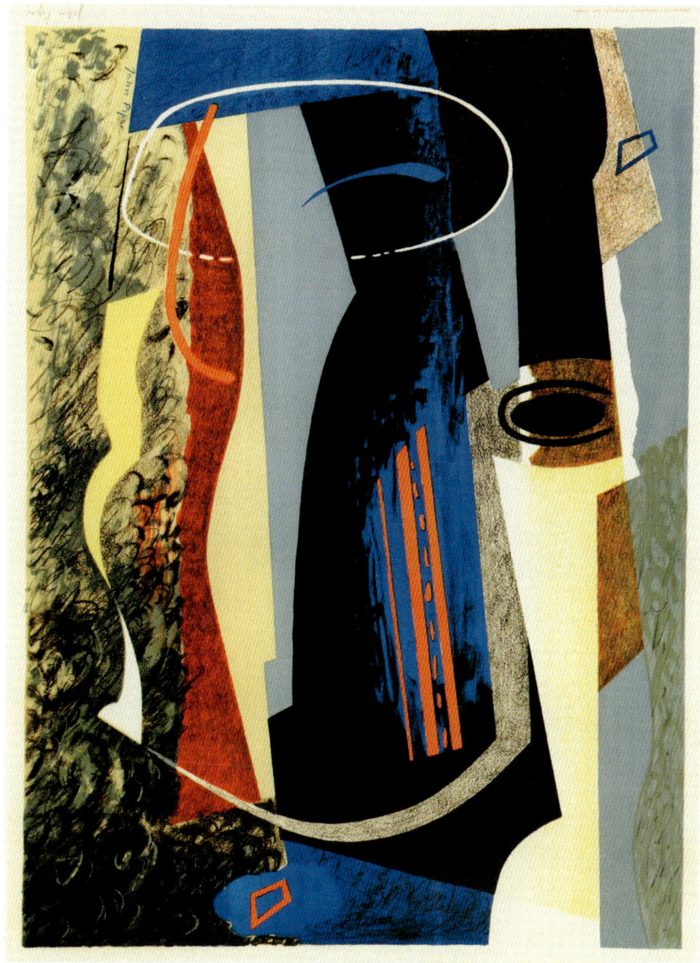

21. *THE THAMES AT CHISWICK*, MARY POTTER (1900-1981)

Mary Potter was born in Beckenham. She started her training at the local art school, winning a scholarship to the RCA but chose to go to the Slade in 1918, where she won a near record number of prizes.

She became an early member of the 7&5 Society but was generally to shun aligning herself with movements. She married Stephen Potter in 1927 and lived on Chiswick Mall painting the domestic world around her with the river in the background; over 100 Chiswick oils are recorded.

During WWII she lived in a farmhouse in Essex, painting portraits but continuing with her still life work. After the war she lived in Harley Street but had to fight for personal time, whilst looking after her family.

She had her first solo exhibition at the Bloomsbury Gallery (1932) followed by two at Tooths (1939 and 1946). During the 50s she showed regularly at the Leicester Galleries.

In 1951 she moved to the Red House, Aldeburgh, Suffolk. She became a close friend of Benjamin Britten with whom she exchanged houses. Eventually Britten constructed a studio for her in his grounds and, with his encouragement, she had her most productive period. From 1967-1980 she had a series of shows at the New Art Centre. The Whitechapel gave her a retrospective (1964). She became an OBE (1980). The Arts Council mounted a retrospective at the Serpentine (1981).

Potter became increasingly abstract in her paintings, (Frances Spalding described her work as 'beginning where words ended', and Kenneth Clark described them as of 'delicate economy'). Her Contemporary Lithograph, produced in her early period, is relatively straightforward, being one of her many views from her Chiswick window. As with many of the artists contributing to Contemporary Lithographs she merely produced a typical work of her genre.

Collections

Tate, Arts Council, public galleries in America, Canada and Australia

References

1964 Exhibition catalogue, *Mary Potter: Paintings 1938-64*, Whitechapel

1981 Exhibition catalogue, *Mary Potter: Paintings 1922-80*, Arts Council

1992 Humphrey Carpenter, *Benjamin Britten*, Faber & Faber

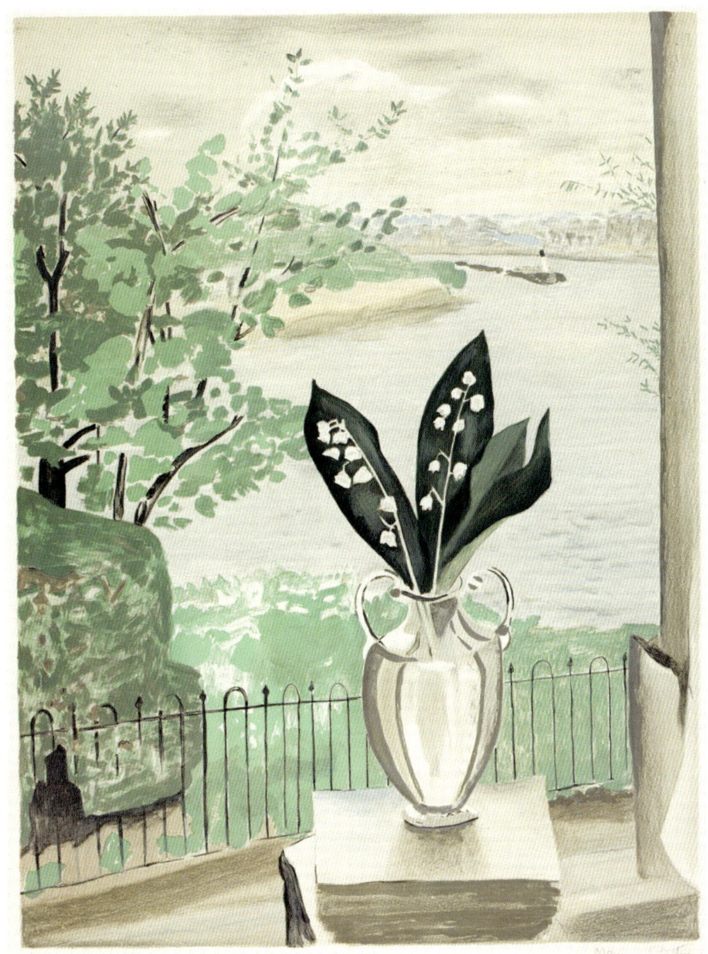

22. *GREENWICH HOSPITAL*, RANDOLPH SCHWABE (1885-1948)

Randolph Schwabe was born in Barton, near Manchester. At 14 he, precociously, attended the RCA but transferred to the Slade (1900-04). He then studied at the Academie Julian, Paris and travelled and worked in Italy.

During WWI he was appointed an Official War Artist, providing drawings on the Home Front.

After the war, he taught at Camberwell and Westminster Schools of Art and at the RCA, before succeeding Tonks at the Slade (1930). He remained as Principal there until his death. He was said to be a gentle teacher and a popular figure in the London art world.

He illustrated a number of books, particularly on historical costume (with Francis Kelly) and on ballet (with Cyril Beaumont). However, he is best known for his topographical scenes, which are more architecturally precise than artistically free flowing. He was a compulsive sketcher, recording wherever he went. He was described in his *Times* obituary as an 'intellectual artist'.

He exhibited continually at NEAC, and the Goupil, Carfax, Leicester and Fine Art galleries.

Schwabe's *Greenwich Hospital* is typical of his many studies of London buildings. Although topographically accurate and done from an interesting angle it can only be described as dull, without colour or movement.

Collections

Imperial War Museum, Tate

References

1951 Exhibition Catalogue, *Randolph Schwabe, memorial exhibition*, Arts Council

1982 Exhibition Catalogue, *Randolph Schwabe 1885-1948*, Fine Art Society

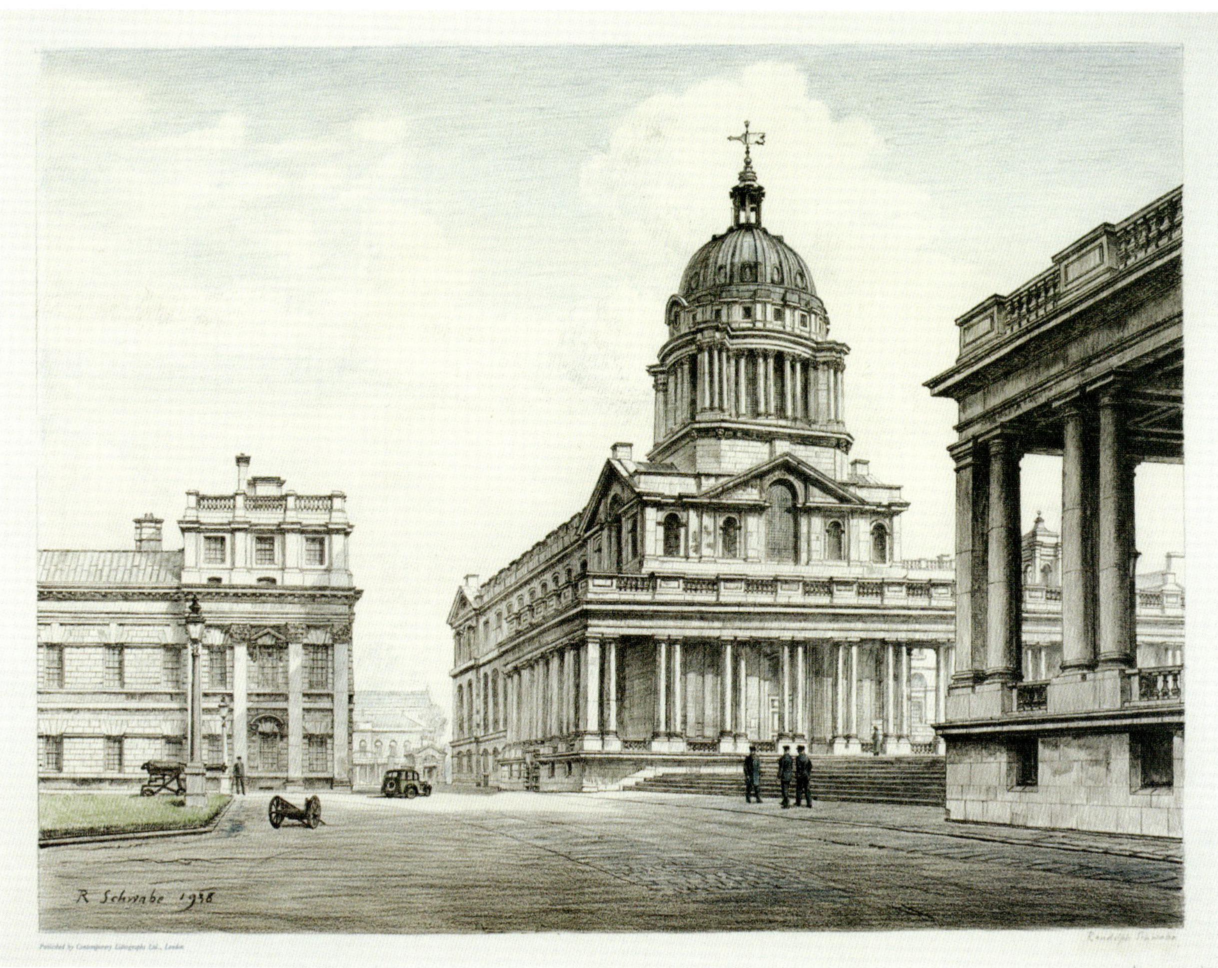
R Schwabe 1938

23. *IMAGINARY HARBOUR*, EDWARD WADSWORTH (1889-1949)

Edward Wadsworth was born in Cleckheaton, West Yorkshire. On his father's death (1921) he was released from the family's mill business and was free to pursue a career as an artist. He went from Bradford School of Art to the Slade (1909). His precocious talent was such that his work was included in Fry's Post-Impressionist exhibition (1913).

Before WWI Wadsworth was caught up in Wyndham Lewis's Vorticist movement and was a signatory to *Blast* (1914). However, after the war, during which he served as a RNVR Intelligence Officer, he broke away from Vorticism. He was briefly allied to Unit One, was bracketed with Nicholson and Hepworth in French avant-garde publications, and contributed to the Pipers' *Axis*. His work, however, became increasingly allied to Surrealism, although he was never a fully 'paid-up' member of the movement.

Early on Wadsworth concentrated on printmaking – woodcuts and lithographs, but dropped all this for tempera painting. His first solo show was at the Adelphi Gallery (1919). He was to show at the Leicester Galleries in the 20s and at Arthur Tooths in the 30s. In 1944 he became an RA, in spite of never having shown there. In 1989 Bradford City Art Gallery mounted a centenary exhibition of his works.

Wadsworth used industrial and nautical motifs throughout his career. In 1926 he produced a book of engravings – *Sailing Ships and Barges of the Western Mediterranean and Adriatic Seas*. His marine still life pictures are of major importance in the history of British modernism. From distant ships he began to concentrate more on detail. He would set up compositions of marine objects in his studio, drawn from his personal collection. His Contemporary Lithograph is a modified version of an *Imaginary Harbour* that he had painted in 1934.

Collections

Tate, V&A and many British galleries.

References

1989 Barbara Wadsworth, *Edward Wadsworth, a painter's life*, Michael Russell

1990 Jeremy Lewison (ed.), *A Genius of Industrial England – Edward Wadsworth 1889-1949*, Arkwright Arts Trust/ Bradford City Art Gallery

2005 Jonathan Black, *Edward Wadsworth, form, feeling and calculation, the complete paintings and drawings*, Philip Wilson

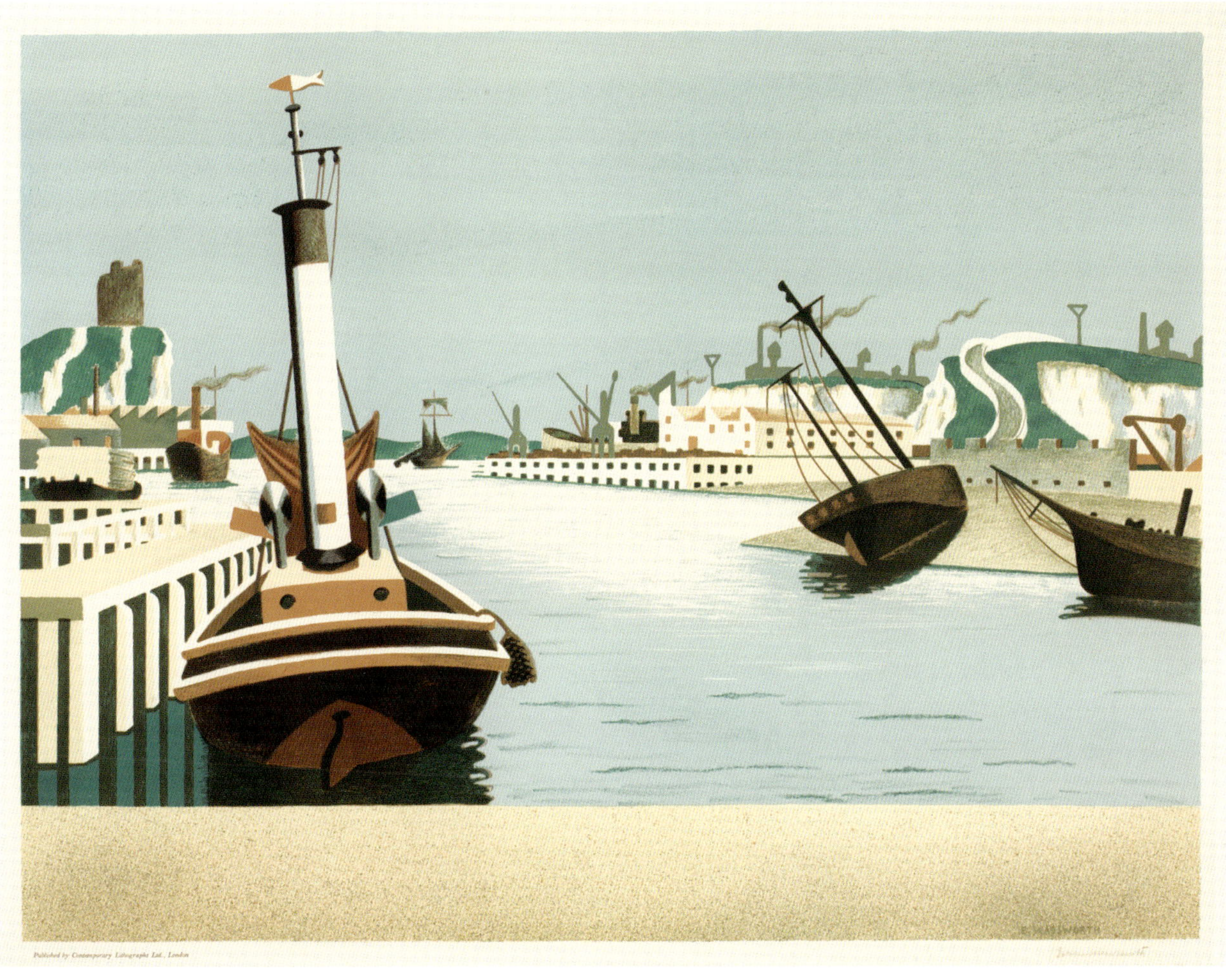

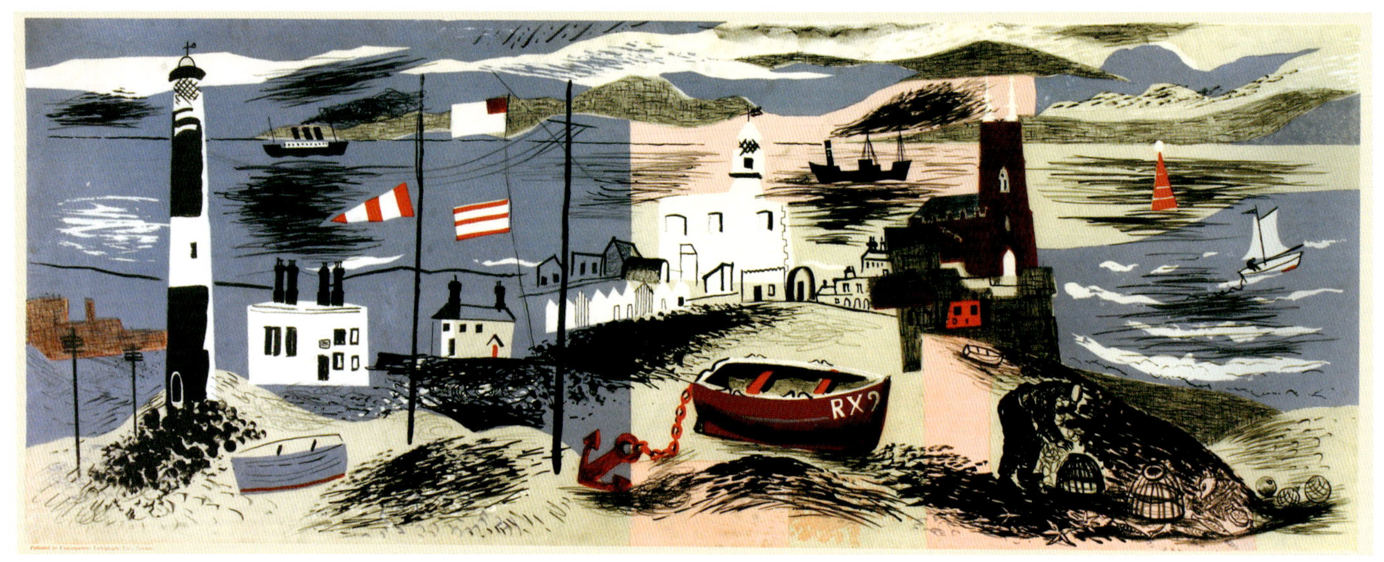

24. *NURSERY FRIEZE – SEASCAPE*, JOHN PIPER (1903-1992)

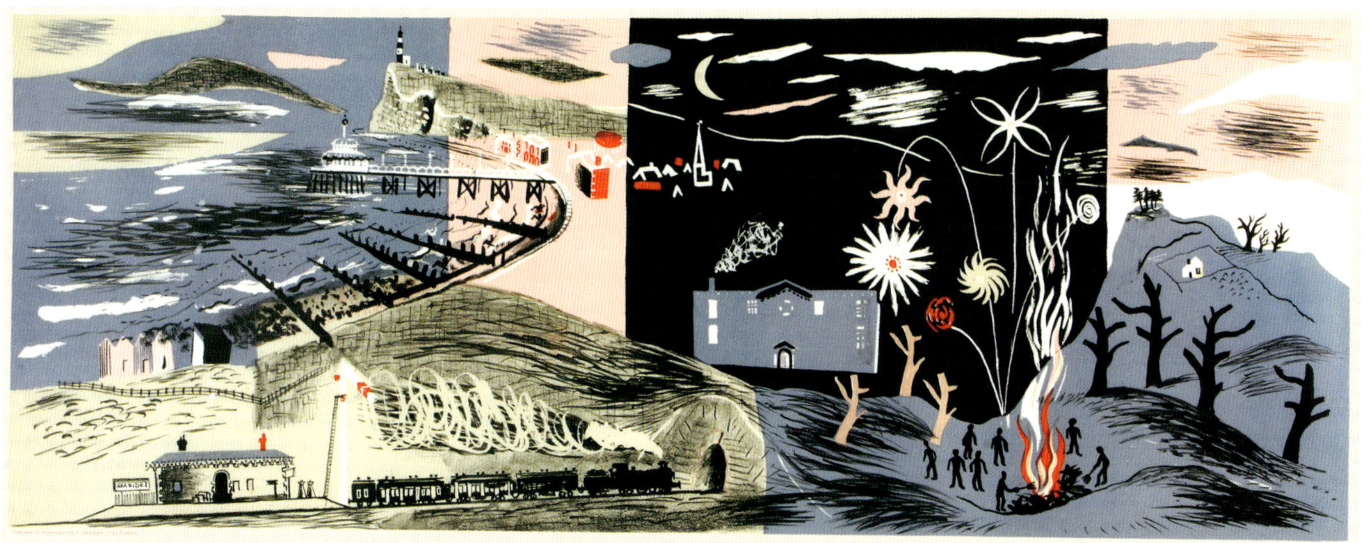

25. *NURSERY FRIEZE – LANDSCAPE*, JOHN PIPER (1903-1992)

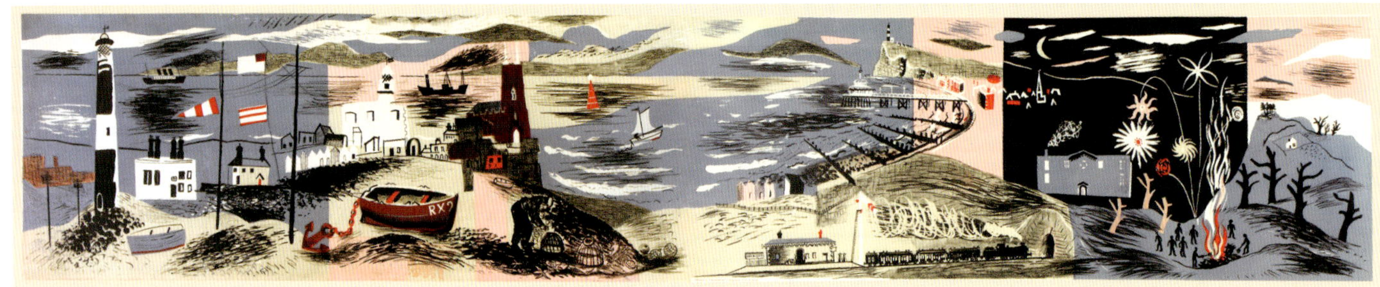
RX

THE PRODUCTION OF THE LITHOGRAPHS

THE PRODUCTION OF THE LITHOGRAPHS

Little has been recorded of how the artists for Contemporary Lithographs were actually briefed or what were the conditions of their commissioning. Roger Berthoud writes facetiously of how Sutherland described his brief – 'Graham was asked to do something specifically for infants schools in place of gnomes on toadstools and fairies coming out of bluebells by Margaret Tarrant, then prevalent'. To us Sutherland's anthropomorphic *Sick Duck* would seem, actually, to be much of the same ilk.

Certainly relatively few of the Contemporary Lithographs have subject matter particularly relevant to children; indeed most of the subjects used were derived from existing work, or from themes preoccupying the artists at the time. This could have been because they were briefed to be 'true' to themselves in what they did. However it may also have been related to pressure from Wellington and Piper to produce to a deadline, from their enthusiasm to see the scheme working and/or because income was needed to be generated quickly given their rather extravagant overheads.

The strongest example of artist preoccupation was probably Paul Nash with the subject of *Megaliths*, for Nash had produced an oil on the subject as early as 1934 (now in the British Council collection). Ruth Clark recalled his first visit to Avebury at the time that Alexander Keiller was working on its reconstruction. 'His response was to the Stones themselves in their quiet setting; his sensitiveness to magic and the similar beauty of monsters was stirred, and he long contemplated the great mass of their forms, their aloofness, their majesty, the shadows they cast upon the grass, the loveliness of their harsh surfaces and the tenderness of their colouring. He seemed to have found renewed vitality in this countryside and in these ancient symbols. At this point of change in his life – they gave an English painter virtue and inspiration'. Clearly Nash was continuing on this personal journey with his Contemporary Lithograph, totally absorbed and totally disregarding the fact that pupils may not, indeed were unlikely to have shared his sensitive spirituality.

Wadsworth, too, produced only a slightly amended version of a previous work – *Imaginary Harbour* which he had produced in 1934. His Contemporary Lithograph removed some parts of the foreground and added others on the horizon to emphasise perpendicular characteristics. Others, if not using or borrowing from previous work, merely produced more of their then current genre – Duncan Grant using a stage scene; Eric Ravilious, a view of Newhaven where he had recently painted with Bawden; Bawden using what Pat Gilmour has referred to as his 'happy cows' speciality; Frances Hodgkins offering one of her abstracted still lifes; Ardizzone doing one of his humorous scenes of London life; and so on. Frances Spalding, in her life of Grant, is fairly dismissive on the subject matter of Contemporary Lithographs overall – 'As with other prints in the series, the choice of subject matter pandered to the English love of the familiar and the anecdotal'. And similarly dismissive are Carey and Griffiths who thought that apart from the lithographs of Piper and Paul Nash – 'the imagery was by no means avant-garde...otherwise largely conventional.'

Perhaps the images in Piper's contributions to the series are most noteworthy, certainly so in terms of his own artistic development. His first Contemporary Lithograph, a strikingly coloured abstract in dashes of brilliant blue and red, was much as he had been producing with the encouragement of Ben Nicholson and Myfanwy Evans. Yet for his other pair of lithographs – the Nursery Friezes *Seascape* and *Landscape* – he seems to have chosen his early interest in the British landscape to which he would return in his essays with John Betjeman for the Shell Guides, and for his own work. It would not be too much of an over-interpretation to see the Nursery Friezes not only as a genuine attempt to appeal to children, but as a personal statement of his breaking with abstraction.

Piper was assigned the role of technical adviser and coach, acting as the go-between the artists and the printers for the production of the Contemporary Lithographs. Yet, in hindsight, it was a curious choice for Piper had barely any experience of auto-lithography, (his first recorded one being *Invention in Colour* published in *Signature* of July 1937). Barnett Freedman, who was one of the commissioned artists, not only was highly skilled in auto-lithography and an evangelist for it, but had a close relationship with the Curwen and was a familiar sight at the Works and was unlikely to find it the 'awful sweat' as Piper was to describe his role. Obviously Piper was the better suited of the Directors to liaise with the Works and Piper experts would point to his experimental attitude to printing in his support. Piper was teaching himself to print from wood before he even went to art school and produced work for the Royal College of Art magazine whilst a student there. But it would have been Piper's practical experience in publishing *Axis*, which had so impressed Oliver Simon, that would have confirmed Piper's suitability for the task ahead. His 'sweat' at Plaistow, rather than deterring him, actually acted as a springboard for his massive lithographic output after WWII.

Robert Medley recalled that 'all the prints were drawn by the artists themselves who went down to the Curwen premises – outlines were drawn on to the main stone and transfers were made to the other stones, which were then drawn with the colour separations'. A few of the artists were experienced in auto-lithography and several more were used to having their pictures produced at the Curwen albeit not by auto-lithography.

Pat Gilmour includes charming snippets characterising some of these artists down at the Works – 'Ravilious really enjoyed the collaboration, Freedman, fierce at times but basically very warm and kindly...John Nash rolling up his sleeves and helping clean up, Ardizzone sharing a pint or a homeward-going bag of fish and chips, Sutherland playing darts during the lunch break, John Piper fondly remembered by Bert Marsh as "a quiet and unassuming man".' John Aldridge described himself as 'wonderfully looked after' by the Curwen craftsmen.

A number of the artists were total novices in auto-lithography – Hitchens, Hodgkins, Sutherland, Aldridge, and, indeed Wadsworth.

Wadsworth described his Contemporary Lithograph as his first in the medium suggesting that previous lithographic prints of his were not executed by him personally. A note from Wadsworth to Wyndham Lewis (19.1.38) seems to confirm this – 'I am not coming up to London next week as I had thought – my debut as a lithographer has been postponed until some time next month'.

Medley's claim that all the artists had auto-lithographed their images has been strongly refuted by Jeremy Greenwood in the case of Bawden. 'Though all the other prints in the first series were indeed auto-lithographs Bawden's *Cattle Market*, the first print in the series, is self-evidently transferred from a lino-cut. Curwen had by then been transferring Bawden's lino-cut images to wallpapers and posters for more than ten years.The precision with which the lino has been cut is untypical of Bawden's other work and it is emphasised by the accuracy of the colour registration. This could only have been achieved by cutting a single lino: the colour separations would then have been made by the craftsmen at the Curwen to Bawden's instructions'.

And certainly Piper's hand was on the work of those new to the medium. Pat Gilmour records of Frances Hodgkins's first efforts – 'She was uncertain, needing encouragement at every stroke. In fact Piper did quite a lot of the print for her and then would encourage her to take the chalk and try again. The result quite transforms the original idea, reversing some of the forms and particularizing a cut-glass ashtray formerly barely hinted at'.

For some of the artists their Contemporary Lithograph was to be their one and only attempt at lithography and they immediately returned to their preferred media, as with Ivon Hitchens. For others, particularly Piper, it was a revelation and a spur to their further experimentation. Helen Binyon considered that for Ravilious 'this introduction to the craft of lithography was the opening of a door. It must have been a great relief to work with colour, after so much black and white engraving…'; and Pat Gilmour confirms this – 'when he eventually started the print, he was immediately enthusiastic about the medium and hopeful of good results'.

Medley was not only inexact in his recall that all the artists auto-lithographed their work, but in that it was all printed at the Curwen Press. By the time the second group of lithographs was to be made Harold Curwen was withdrawing from the Press due to a nervous breakdown. At least half the second series was done at the Baynard Press under the watchful eye of Thomas Griffits. Griffits was every bit as enthusiastic about, as skilled in, and as hands-on with, lithography as Harold Curwen. However, his management style was quite opposite. Whereas Curwen trusted his artists and gave them encouragement and freedom, Griffits was likely to take over the job and dictate what was to happen. Piper would have been no match for him.

Piper's two Nursery Friezes had to be produced at Waterlows as they were too wide for the Curwen presses. Here Piper found a different atmosphere again. At both Curwen and Baynard the union chapels had been won over by a variety of arguments such as that bringing in artists would up the reputation of the firm and therefore bring in more work which would be to everyone's advantage. At Waterlows Piper found himself tucked away in an upstairs warehouse room covered in cobwebs because there had been union murmurs at the possibility that new non-union staff were being taken on.

The first series was ready for exhibition in January 1937; the second series was issued in March 1938.

Although the intention was for each lithograph to have a 400 print edition, Ann Baer was not at all sure that this was actually carried through, and this doubt makes it difficult to judge the relative success of each series, and, indeed, of each lithograph.

And there is a similar lack of records about artists' signatures. Although the second lot of publicity declares each print 'hand-signed' some seem to have been signed on the plate and on the print, some on the one but not the other, and some not at all.

Bibliography

1936 Paul Nash, *Experiments in colour reproductions*, Penrose Annual 38

1939 Jan Gordon, *Contemporary Lithographs*, Penrose Annual 41

1955 Anthony Bertram, *Paul Nash, the portrait of an artist*, Faber & Faber

1973 Margot Eates, *Paul Nash 1889-1946*, John Murray

1982 Roger Berthoud, *Graham Sutherland, a biography*, Faber & Faber

1983 Helen Binyon, *Eric Ravilious, memoir of an artist*, Frederic C.Beil

1989 Barbara Wadsworth, *Edward Wadsworth, a painter's life*, London

2006 Ian Rogerson, *Barnett Freedman, the graphic art*, The Fleece Press

THE LAUNCH

THE LAUNCH

The Contemporary Lithographs were issued in two series. The first was exhibited at the Curwen Gallery, 108 Great Russell Street in January 1937.

Simon's office was at No.108 so it was possible that this was a space hired specifically for the occasional show. If there was a catalogue it hasn't survived; but an undated eight-page illustrated brochure must have been issued soon afterwards. This was entitled *Lithographs for Schools* and along with general blurb as to the purpose of the scheme and the prices (different for education and the general public), were three quotes from reviews variously in the *Architectural Review* (January 1937), *The New Statesman & Nation* (23 January 1937) and *The Times* (23 January 1937). As with the boards outside West End theatres, the parts of these reviews included in the brochure read more like hypes than measured commentary.

The authors of the brochure, presumably Wellington and Piper, selected from the *Architectural Review* congratulations on the chosen medium – 'The choice of lithography as a medium has entirely justified itself'; from *The New Statesman & Nation* they extracted parts which argued for giving children 'modern' pictures rather than old masters; and from the *The Times* they chose the emphasis on 'originality' – 'an autographic version of an original picture must always be preferable to a reproduction mechanically produced…'; all three quotes underlying, in sales jargon, the USP (unique selling points) of the series as they saw them – quality, accessibility and originality.

These characteristics were further highlighted in a four-sided letter-press leaflet which contained further tributes, this time from art and education world notables – Kenneth Clark (then Director of the National Gallery), W.G.Constable (of the Courtauld Institute), P.H.Jowett (of the Royal College of Art), and Sir Michael Sadler (late Master of University College, Oxford); and then, in addition, two people who had been more closely in contact with the scheme, Marion Richardson (London County Council Inspector of Art) and, inevitably, Henry Morris. Griffiths considered all of these solicited, rather than dispassionate, reviewers. Kenneth Clark pointed to the 'life-enhancing' quality of contemporary art for the young; Morris, embarrassingly hyped the event of the series as 'one of the most significant happenings in English education since the war'; Jowett, from his own standpoint, saw the series as 'an opportunity for artists to place their work before a wider public'; only Constable introduced any doubt as to the wonder of the enterprise stating that although all the prints were interesting and stimulating 'some were better than others'.

A more objective comment, with hindsight, was later included in the Dartington Hall Trustees report on the Visual Arts in 1946 (proposing the Design Council and the Arts Council) – 'The reception of the prints expectedly varied from enthusiasm by more progressive authorities and directors of education to the ribaldry of supplies-officers accustomed to buying from furnishing firms'.

Lithographs
for
Schools

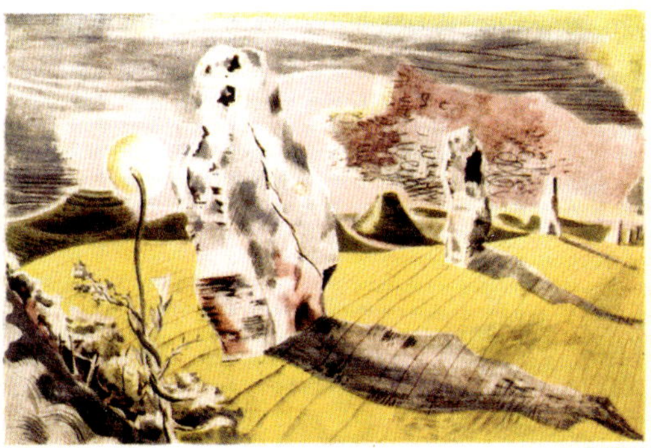

Landscape of the megaliths — Paul Nash

Contemporary Lithographs, Ltd.,
(Directors: JOHN PIPER and ROBERT WELLINGTON)
15, Soho Square, London, W.1
Telephone: GERrard 1139

Prospectus for Contemporary Lithographs Ltd - First Series

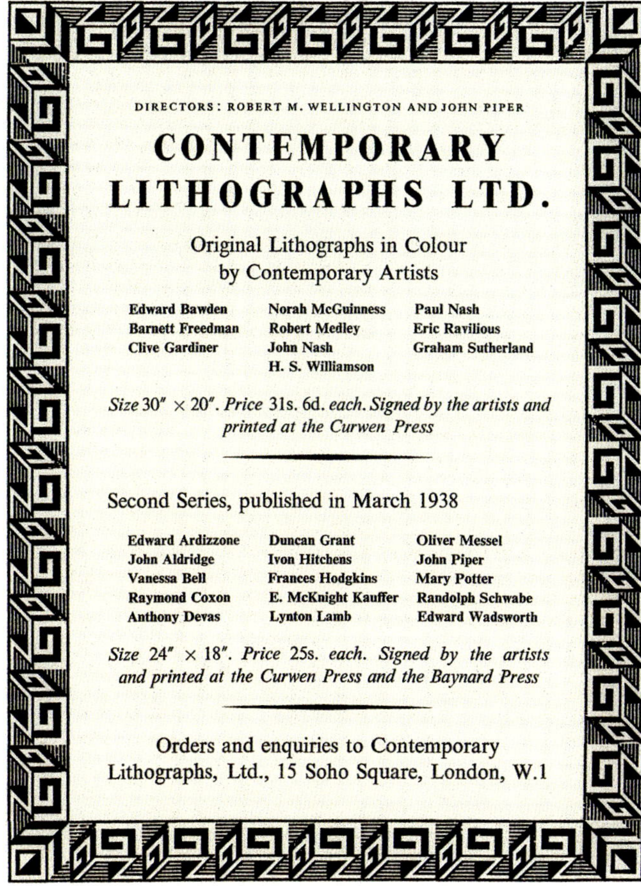

Contemporary Lithographs Ltd advertisement in *Signature* magazine, March 1938

Wellington and Piper had been relatively successful in getting their chosen artists to agree to take part in their scheme, although an advertisement for the prints in *Signature* named McKnight Kauffer and Oliver Messel as taking part, and one can only wonder why that didn't happen. Griffiths points out that Vincent Lines was included in the second series but does not feature in the *Signature* advertisement, perhaps being a last minute fill-in for the missing Kauffer and Messel. And with Simon and Curwen on their side, things went reasonably well in the production of the prints, mainly produced at the Plaistow Works. However when it came to marketing, sales and distribution the commercial naivety of the pair became apparent, especially where education was concerned,

Wellington recalled the first sales tour he made with Ree – 'It was an abysmal failure. We failed to interest anyone. We tried Leicester, Birmingham, Manchester and Worcester without success. The idea and the artists were too novel, and considered too advanced'. Brenda Rawnsley was to experience a similar response with her 'School Prints', some dozen years later, when she triumphantly offered Moore, Matisse, Dufy, Braque, Léger and Picasso to English educational authorities.

Medley's account of a trip he and Graham Sutherland made to try to sell the prints to the headmasters of Clifton College and Bristol Grammar Schools, a rather more select target than that of Wellington and Ree, reads more like a boyish spree than the implementation of a well-thought out marketing strategy. The two of them shared the driving of Sutherland's MG sports car, of which he was inordinately proud – 'We used to take turns at the wheel, and he always managed a couple of miles an hour better than I did over a set distance. But it was his car!' The focus of their energies seems questionable and Clifton College and Bristol Grammar School hardly representative for the democratisation of art, certainly not as Henry Morris would have seen it. It was J.E.Barton, the headmaster of Bristol Grammar School who had provided them with the glowing report of the first series, which had appeared in the *Architectural Review*. All was very cosy but not to further commercial success.

The sales target for the first series was very definitely schools, although the public were encouraged to buy, at a dearer rate. With little success with the first series, by the time the second series was launched the prints were aimed clearly at the general public – *Original Prints by Living Artists* was the title of the leaflet produced advertising all 25 prints. The educational concern of Contemporarty Lithographs Ltd was clear in their evangelically argued introduction –

> 'The ambition of Contemporary Lithographs Ltd is to introduce the work of living artists to the general public IN THE ORIGINAL. Has the artist a place in twentieth century life, as the author and the musician obviously have? To the majority, the painter or sculptor is a strange and suspicious character; Epstein is mistrusted even more than Shaw. More humiliating, an English painter like Wilson Steer, O.M. is comparatively unknown among a public which would be ashamed to admit ignorance of Thomas Hardy or Edward Elgar.

> Yet there is a large enough potential public for contemporary art. The trouble is that only a fractional minority have the opportunity of seeing any original examples for themselves, much less of hanging them on their own walls. There is practically no machinery for 'getting pictures across' to a public comparable with that existing for music and literature. An original oil or water-colour painting, costing anything between ten and ten thousand pounds, is a luxury beyond the normal scope of households whose yearly income lies between three hundred and fifteen hundred pounds. To make original modern pictures available to a wide public some cheaper form is clearly necessary'.

Again they stress the originality of the auto-lithographed print –

> 'It is a process of reproduction in which the prints are taken directly from the artist's original work. This means there is no loss of vitality, and no intervention by a second person or a camera, translating the artist's work into terms of another medium. The lithographic print is an original, faithful to the artist's conception and printed in his colours'.

Contemporary Lithographs Ltd, as with School Prints Ltd, faced with a commercial disaster, turn to the interior decorator for help. *Homes and Gardens*, *Vogue*, and the like, were courted in a desperate bid to disperse their rapidly accumulating stock.

To get wider publicity an exhibition, of all 25 published prints, was mounted at the Leicester Galleries in September–October 1938. The small 8-page leaflet for this has a preface in the form of an open letter from Sir Michael Sadler to John Piper, along with the reprinted text of the second brochure.

Efforts were made to get print retailers to stock the lithographs. Jan Gordon, in his article in the *Penrose Annual* for 1939, writes scathingly of such outlets – "There can be but little doubt that some of the poor response of the normal Briton to art must be found in the almost incredibly low quality of art appreciation shown by the general distributors, that is by most of the shops that specialise in art prints and framing... and yet this is the filter through which Contemporary Lithographs must pass before they can reach the public on anything like an effective scale'.

The pair also seem to have tried other means of advertising the prints more widely. One example was the appearance of John Aldridge's *The Mill in Essex* as an illustrated page in the prestigious *Country Life Annual 1938* (printed at the Curwen) with the accompanying blurb – 'From a lithograph by the artist for Contemporary Lithographs Ltd. One of a series of twenty-two prints by living artists recently exhibited at the Leicester Galleries, London', The contents page of the annual gives the lithographs as 'the enterprise of Robert Wellington and John Piper'.

In spite of Wellington's and Piper's declared intent to produce new series annually there is no evidence that any further sets were even in preparation before market nervousness at the impending war hit all commercial operations. Griffiths quotes Piper as seeing the War as more of a help than an hindrance as it enabled the pair to delay paying the bills a little longer. Certainly they were in financial trouble as in a

Original Prints by living Artists

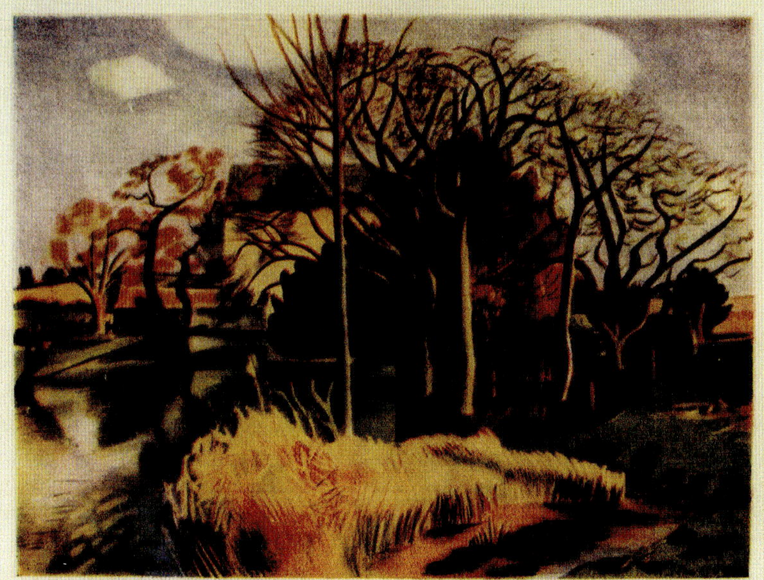

John Aldridge *Mill in Essex*

CONTEMPORARY LITHOGRAPHS Ltd.

Directors: *JOHN PIPER and ROBERT WELLINGTON*

15 Soho Square, London, W.1 GERrard 1139

Prospectus aimed at the general public

letter to Barnett Freedman, (who tended to build up quite bulky correspondences with many of his commissioning agents on the matter of payment), Wellington wrote explaining that the sum of £5.3s, which was owed to the artist couldn't be paid 'at the moment'.

Medley puts the main blame for the failure of Contemporary Lithographs Ltd on the British public, and its unwillingness to patronise anything unfamiliar. He, like. Gordon, also pans the distributors. Elspeth Moncrieff, in her article in *Edward Bawden, editioned prints* likewise criticises the public and the distributors not so much for their prejudice against the subject matter but for their inability 'to understand the difference between an original print and a reproduction'. The confusion as to what was an 'original' and what not was to haunt later lithographic series. The issue was not only to what extent had machinery and printers intervened in the making of an auto-lithographed print, but also as to how 'limited' was a limited edition; thirty copies each carefully lifted from the press by the artist him- or herself – yes; four hundred lifted by other hands – doubtful.

Ann Baer saw Wellington and Piper as a pair of idealistic, optimistic amateurs, well-intentioned but totally unbusinesslike. She felt that Wellington had flung himself into the enterprise in the spirit of 'what fun!' – ostrich-like in relation to war looming, imagining that what they liked others would like, and blind to the fact that the general public was suspicious of anything that wasn't totally representational, and greeting abstraction with derision.

Medley's summing up of Wellington, the major player in the whole operation, was kindly but damning: 'What had made him the imaginative, understanding and optimistic impresario for artists had not equipped him with a corresponding business sense. Left to himself, the optimism became a Micawberish inability to distinguish between asset and overdraft'.

Bibliography

Prospectuses

Lithographs for Schools, Contemporary Lithographs Ltd, V&A Art Library (Box III 94A)

1938 Letterpress leaflet of 10 tributes, inserted into copy of 1938 Contemporary Lithographs Ltd brochure in V&A Art Library

1938 *Original Prints by Living Artists*, Contemporary Lithographs Ltd, V&A Art Library (Box I 94BB)

Reviews

January 1937 J.E.Barton, *Architectural Review*, LXXXI

23 January 1937 Clive Bell, *The New Statesman & Nation*, p120

22 February 1937, *The Times*, p17

Exhibition catalogues

1938 Leicester Galleries September - October (no.681 of Galleries numbering)

THE AFTERMATH

THE AFTERMATH

Although the onset of WWII (schools evacuated in temporary accommodation, Wellington, Piper and their associates drafted into more essential work etc.) would be the last straw for the financially teetering Contemporary Lithographs Ltd. Wellington, with his early success at Zwemmer's, had, perhaps, been naively optimistic in thinking his skills, charm and enthusiasm would be easily transferable to other markets; what worked with art lovers who would personally journey to the Mecca that Zwemmer's became, failed when it came to local education authorities' supplies officers. Wellington and Piper perhaps should have taken noticed of Barnett Freedman's advice 'Let every man be his own lithographer but have the business of distribution taken out of his hands'.

An additional problem, perhaps more so when Contemporary Lithographs were targeted at the general public rather than just schools, was one of 'originality' – what constituted an 'original' print? Arguments about originality of prints had previously reached a court of law, in the case of Pennell, Whistler and Sickert, and were to dog some of the later series, particularly in relation to the prints produced for Brenda Rawnsley by the European artists, for the third series of School Prints. The publicity *Original Prints by Living Artists* put out by Wellington and Piper did just not ring true enough for the market. (see Appendix).

The bombing of the Contemporary Lithographs Ltd offices early in the war (Baer dates this 1940, Griffiths 1941) was the nail in the coffin. The unsold and undamaged stock (Griffths estimates this as a large amount of the original production) was housed, for the rest of the war, in the basement of the *New Statesman & Nation* offices, 10 Gt Turnstile. At first this seems to have been nothing more than a friendly arrangement between Wellington and John Roberts, then the manager of the *New Statesman*. In 1946 Roberts set up a publishing company, the Turnstile Press, as an associated activity for the *Statesman*. Eventually he agreed to start selling the remaining Contemporary Lithographs Ltd stock via the Press. Ann Baer, who was working for the Press, was assigned the role of sales person and told – 'You know about this art stuff Ann. You take over'; which she did. She had studied for a time at Chelsea College of Art and this was deemed sufficient for the task; certainly she knew more about prints compared to anyone else employed at the time.

The Turnstile Press offices were above those of the *New Statesman*, in Gt Turnstile, off Lincoln's Inn Fields. Ann Baer has described how she went about marketing and selling the lithographs –

'By putting small advertisements in the *New Statesman*, I sold quantities of the lithographs by post or to members of the public who came puffing up the staircase to buy them'. She seems to have been most effective in using the *New Statesman* as a selling vehicle and she was certainly helped by the fact that paper was rationed, new prints rare, and importing prints from the continent impossible; good new prints had become highly desirable commodities. Griffiths reports finding a Turnstile Press price list stating that only five of the first series were still available (at two guineas each) and only eleven of the second (at one and a half guineas each); the difference in price related to difference in size.

When the sale of the lithographs was transferred to the *New Statesman* there was no listing of quantities so that if only a few of one print was available it was impossible to know whether it had been a good seller, or whether its numbers had been reduced by fire and water when the Soho Square premises were bombed. Ann Baer recalls only ever handling a few of the Ravilious and the John Nash. She recalls the Hitchens and the Hodgkins as tending to be bought by the more sophisticated buyers. The least popular were the Schwabe and the McGuiness for their lack of colour, the Piper abstract as being altogether too modern, and Lines's *Skaters* too roughly sketched and printed in insipid colours.

One curious sale to Brazil came about by a rich Australian, Ted Dyason, retaining Bernhard Baer to buy prints for a museum in São Paulo, which he supported and a number of the Contemporary Lithographs are lodged there, presumably to this day. At the time overseas sales did not attract purchase tax which made the prints relatively attractive there.

Ann Baer found considerable difficulty in liaising with Wellington, partly because he was working night shifts as a news writer at the BBC and slept during the day. But timing was only one of her problems with Wellington. Her sophisticated diplomacy and self-confidence in her selling role come across in her record of their relationship –

'I soon discovered that his one business principle was never to answer letters, so I used to send him letters starting "I propose...and unless I hear to the contrary by next week I will put this into operation". As I never did hear, I was able to manage everything to my own satisfaction.'

The *New Statesman*, with Lund Humphries, set up, alongside the Turnstile Press, their own fine art reproducing firm – The Ganymed Press (1947), next door to the Statesman's offices. Ann Baer was transferred over to run it. It issued its first catalogue in 1950 offering its own prints. In addition to this Ganymed took commissions for reproductions from major public galleries. The selling of the remaining Contemporary Lithographs went, with Ann Baer, to Ganymed as it was seen to be a more appropriate selling base than the Turnstile Press. By then sales were drying up and she, of necessity, had to concentrate her efforts on Ganymed. Ganymed was to go through a number of metamorphoses before being sold to the Medici Society (1980).

Apart from the problem of liaising with Wellington Ann Baer dealt with the modest flow out of Contemporary Lithograph prints with ease and efficiency. There seems to have been only one blip when Roland of Roland, Browse & Delbanco mistakedly accused her of poaching his exclusive arrangement with the Munich print maker Piper Drucke when she advertised that she was selling Pipers!

With the sale of Ganymed the remaining Contemporary Lithograph Ltd stock was returned to Wellington at his home, Ashford Chase, a great Lutyens House near Petersfield, in Hampshire. Final debts of the company were said to have been cleared by Piper, and by Wellington's family. Medley records Wellington as having been rescued by his brother (later Sir) Lindsey Wellington. Whether the 'rescue' was more than financial Medley does not specify, but whatever its nature, Wellington soon found himself, during the war, working in the newsroom of the BBC. His job there was described, by Medley, as 'deciding upon what we ought or ought not to be told'.

At some point Wellington appears to have left the BBC to join CEMA (the Council for Education in Music and the Arts), the precursor of the Arts Council. He was to be its first exhibition officer, This would not only have made good use of his Zwemmer years but would bring the crusading element of Contemporary Lithographs Ltd to it in that CEMA's aim was educational, in the case of Wellington's role again, 'to bring art to the people'. CEMA/Arts Council was to build up a considerable collection of contemporary works of art and, by the end of the war, had already opened two galleries in London to act as show windows for exhibitions that they would tour around the country. With CEMA records being sparse there is no account of how successful Wellington was to be in democratising art in this context.

That Wellington's fervour for campaigns and projects furthering art remained with him into retirement is exemplified by his trying to run a sort of artists' colony at Ashford Close; this had no greater success than his 'art for education' Contemporary Lithographs Ltd. He was living in the gatehouse to the grand Lutyen's Ashford Chase owned by Lord Horder and seems to have taken a hand in developing and administering the estate. He is remembered as a man of great charm and sophistication, highly knowledgeable about contemporary art with a wide artistic social network, but perhaps not cut out for commercial enterprises, however modest. He died 2nd July 1990.

John Piper seems to have found in the minor designing of his *Nursery Friezes* and the major onset of WWII some kind of release allowing him to be true to his early love of architecture and landscape and his earlier style of romantic/magical representation. Frances Spalding provides further clues as to Piper's change of heart from his championing of abstraction to becoming the leading topographical artist of his time – first his need to have a more solid income with the birth of his first child, secondly, his nostalgia with the threat of war and possible damage to Britain's cultural heritage, and thirdly his meeting John Betjeman.

Piper met Betjeman in 1937 having been recommended to him by J.M.Richards of the *Architectural Review*. In hindsight, some of Piper's adolescent notebooks as a church crawler are said to have an uncanny resemblance to the early *Shell Guides*. Betjeman was thought not to have been aware of the notebooks when he initially commissioned Piper to work on some of Shell's vastly popular, but rather eccentric, *Guides*. In 1937 Piper compiled the *Guide to Oxfordshire*, and 1939 found him touring with Betjeman to produce one on Shropshire. Gradually Piper became more involved until eventually, when Betjeman tired of the project, Piper was to become its editor. He was to be associated with the *Guides* until 1980. The *Guides* gave Piper greater scope for his interest in landscape and building, and in photography as well as art. This was furthered when he was appointed an Official War

Artist and involved in the 'Recording Britain' project.

After the war, along with his burgeoning use of the lithographic print to produce his imaginative buildings in their landscapes, Piper began his association with Benjamin Britten. Britten first met the Pipers at a rowdy meeting on the future of the Group Theatre at Piper's Oxfordshire farmhouse. From 1946 onwards Piper was to collaborate on the majority of Britten's operas providing magical stage sets and costume designs. These more decorative essays spread to Piper working with stained glass and ceramics in the 50s and 60s, and his later work with tapestry.

As one of Britain's leading post-war artists Piper received a Companion of Honour (1972) and was given retrospectives by the Arts Council (1953) and at MOMA, Oxford (1979). Piper's life revolved around his art; his perhaps 'adopted by association' evangelistic streak, first with Myfanwy and abstract art, and then with Wellington and the Contemporary Lithographs, was a relatively short-lived period in his long creative career. That his prints were to become some of the most popular hung on the walls of people's homes was not by intent, but by Piper's own enthusiasm for romantic ruins hitting a nostalgic market stream.

Henry Morris, however, was to continue with his evangelism of art as being central to living, through to the end. After the war, whilst continuing with his village colleges, Morris took on a number of advisory roles to education and to government, one of the most pertinent being Cultural Adviser to the Minister responsible for Town Planning.

Whether this position was cause or effect, Morris came up with a scheme to run a cultural centre from a pub in South Hatfield. When this failed to take off he put forward an idea for an artists' colony – the provision of cheap accommodation for artists and craftsmen – with the proviso that they could prove they were contributing to the wider community. James McComb, of Hatfield and Welwyn New Towns, worked along with Morris to implement his scheme, which became the Digswell Arts Trust. The first occupants arrived in 1957; by 1959, when Digswell was formally opened, there were fifteen artists in residence.

Of the many artists benefiting from Digswell, one of the best known was Hans Coper, the potter; he found life so congenial there he stayed for some five years. Morris's enthusiasm for the scheme was such that he left his grand residence in Cambridge for an altogether more modest dwelling in Welwyn itself. This was something of a mixed blessing for Digswell as Morris was wont to make frequent visits of inspection! Morris received a CBE for his pioneering work in education (1942). He died in December 1961.

As was noted, in describing the production of Contemporary Lithographs, Harold Curwen's breakdown and withdrawal from the Press meant that some of the second series were printed at the Baynard Press. Although Curwen had retired from the Press by 1939, many of his artists were to continue to consult him on printing matters, particularly on lithography, such was his expertise, enthusiasm and the esteem he had attracted. His 'spirit of joy' in good design for printing was to cascade down to other generations. Curwen opened a small village shop, a retirement dream of many who have an image of idyllic rural life. He died suddenly in 1949, at the young age of 63. His achievement in breaking down the snob barrier between book and fine print production and commercial printing, and of elevating the standard of British printing all round, was recognised, posthumously when the Double Crown Club devoted its 219th dinner, in 1973, entirely to his honour.

Oliver Simon continued in his Directorship of the Curwen Press and paralleled his work there with his editorship of *Signature*, which ran to 1954. He put his advanced ideas on book design into a book – *An Introduction to Typography* (1945). As with Curwen, Simon's pioneering work was celebrated posthumously at the Double Crown Club dinner on the 26th April 1956 when the Club mounted an exhibition of the books for which Simon had been responsible (along with celebrating his passion for cricket and his expertise as a player!).

There is no evidence to suggest that later schemes for lithographic series 'for the people' were actually directly influenced by Wellington and Piper's Contemporary Lithographs. Brenda Rawnsley, the entrepreneur behind 'The School Prints' (from 1946), the only one of the later schemes with the initial motivation of improving pupils' aesthetic awareness, was fulfilling the socially motivated ideas of her young husband, killed in the war. She reports of only vaguely being aware of previous similar projects. Yet Contemporary Lithographs could well have added, along with the AIA prints, to the general zeitgeist for the post-war popularisation of art through lithographic prints with the School Prints, the Lyons Lithographs, and the Festival of Britain series.

Several of the Contemporary Lithographs images have become iconic, for fine print collectors, such as Ravilious's 'Newhaven Harbour', attracting high prices, ironically, in that they were produced to combat elitism. Nevertheless, Griffiths, one of the foremost print experts, rates the Contemporary Lithographs as being a landmark in British 20th century printmaking, a pioneer in raising the standards of aesthetic appreciation in the general public.

Bibliography

1981 Bernhard Baer, *Ganymed: printing, publishing, design*, V&A

1999 Ann Baer, *Ganymed*, Matrix 19

2006 Ruth Artmonsky, *The School Prints, A Romantic Project*, Artmonsky Arts

2007 Charlie Batchelor, *Tea and a Slice of Art*, Artmonsky Arts

APPENDIX

APPENDIX

THE AUTO-LITHOGRAPHIC PRINT - AN ORIGINAL?

The publicity leaflet for the whole series of Contemporary Lithographs was headed *Original Prints by Living Artists.* Arguments as to whether such prints could justify the epithet 'original' was to dog them, and following series, particularly the 'European' six from the School Prints. The matter was crucial because if these prints could be seen as authentic works of art to be treasured as 'by the artist's own hand' this would seriously improve their marketability.

Harold Curwen and Barnett Freedman were foremost in pushing the 'originality' of an auto-lithographed print, and there was a trail of supporters arguing along similar lines.

'But when all is said and done, nothing can take the place of an artist working in a medium which he thoroughly understands, producing marks on a flat surface which go straight into the printing press, without "let or hindrance".'
Barnett Freedman, *Signature* No.2 March 1936

'...when the experienced artist makes his own drawing with lithographic materials, every print is an original.'
Harold Curwen in *Autolithography*, Penrose Annual 1938

'Above all, the result so obtained, can be multiplied indefinitely: each example will be an original work of art, in the sense it will be precisely as it left the artist's hand, without interposition of any mechanical means of production.'
Quoted in *Barnett Freedman*, Art & Technics 1947

'...the process is more like that by which an artist produces a painting by continually correcting and perfecting his design until it approaches something of his original conception. This attitude to lithographic design is the only one which allows any choice of arriving at a true use of the medium, so that one can say of a print "This is a work of art and a thing that makes the most of the delightful qualities of lithography".'
Edwin La Dell, 'Autolithography at the RCA', *The Penrose Annual* 1952

'Autolithographic prints give the true value of every touch of the artist and represent the only method of duplication in which there is no interference between the artist and the finished print'.
Thomas Griffits, *The Rudiments of Lithography*, 1956

'At its best, it is one of the greatest media of direct creative expression and one of the few which an artist can use to see his work reproduced in limitless numbers without the smallest infringement of the original design'.
Robin Darwin, foreword to Griffits book 1956

Peter Floud, in *Image 3* (1950) scathingly challenges auto-lithographers to specify what exactly are their indefinable qualities of texture and depth that only artists can produce, that lithographic printers can't. And Griffiths, who applauds Floud's scepticism, challenges along similar lines – 'Usually the only way to distinguish the images that the artist worked on from those that craftsmen created from their (the artists') maquettes is by the greater technical incompetence of the former'.

The elements to the auto-lithography protagonist's argument seem to be the natural free-flowing creativity of the medium, that no hand touches the print except that of the artist, and that no photo-mechanisation is involved.

Whether it is a more natural, spontaneous medium for printing than etching or engraving, seems irrelevant to the 'originality' problem. Obviously working on a flat surface, just as if one were drawing or painting, with a pliable crayon, is more 'free' than working with an engraver's tool. But even if spontaneity were to be considered an aspect of 'originality', Floud and Griffiths have the riposte of where does freedom of creativity lie when it comes to colour auto-lithography, which was the medium for the Contemporary Lithographs. The separation on the stones or plates of the different colours and the difficulty of colour overlaps is the reverse of straightforward for the artist. Many lithographic printers would have argued that artists just do not understand colour combinations as they did (although there could have been a union defensiveness about the intrusion of artists at the Works in this assessment).

On the matter of 'no other human hand', Floud and Griffiths point out that when autolithography is for mass distribution with 400 or so of each Contemporary Lithograph (4000 for the European School Prints), the artist must inevitably yield to the printing machine and cannot hope to see his work through to completion. The auto-lithographic artist may have eliminated the lithographic printer but still had to use the commercial machine minder.

Not only was the commercial printer necessary to produce large quantities of a print but photo-mechanisation for colour lithography made it cheaper. Carey and Griffiths maintain that it was the introduction of photo- mechanisation, so essential for the mass production of original material, that was to destroy any alliance that the likes of Curwen and Griffits had had with auto-lithographic artists.

Further Floud maintained that often it was difficult for anyone to tell whether a print was auto-lithographed or not and that the general public certainly couldn't, nor, in most cases, didn't care how a print was produced as long as it served its decorative purpose to please.

And then there is the matter of exclusivity that strengthens the claim of originality for studio – rather than works – produced prints – prints that were limited in number and each signed by the artist and presumably each pulled by the artist. Whereas Wellington and Piper, and later, Brenda Rawnsley, had difficulty in selling their 'original' mass-produced prints made at the works with the help of the printers, 'artist's prints', studio produced, were to start a boom from the 1950s.

The general opinion, nowadays, seems to be that the print series of the 30s, 40s and 50s, contributing to the 'art for everyone' ethos of the time, cannot be described as 'original' neither from a technical, nor a market view point. Wellington and Piper's attempt to sell their Contemporary Lithographs as originals was easily seen through, whereas Ann Baer's selling them for what they were, well produced prints, proved altogether more successful. (She modestly claims her relative success was due more to the post-war optimism). Whether Wellington's and Piper's rather weak originality claim detracted from sales or not takes nothing away from the fact that the Contemporary Lithographs are generally rated the best quality of the various lithographic series of the mid-century by content, style and, above all, quality of printing.